Cambridge Elements ≡

Elements in the Philosophy of Immanuel Kant
edited by
Desmond Hogan
Princeton University
Howard Williams
University of Cardiff
Allen Wood
Indiana University

THE POLITICS OF BEAUTY

A Study Of Kant's Critique Of Taste

Susan Meld Shell
Boston College

CAMBRIDGE
UNIVERSITY PRESS

CAMBRIDGE
UNIVERSITY PRESS

University Printing House, Cambridge CB2 8BS, United Kingdom

One Liberty Plaza, 20th Floor, New York, NY 10006, USA

477 Williamstown Road, Port Melbourne, VIC 3207, Australia

314–321, 3rd Floor, Plot 3, Splendor Forum, Jasola District Centre,
New Delhi – 110025, India

103 Penang Road, #05–06/07, Visioncrest Commercial, Singapore 238467

Cambridge University Press is part of the University of Cambridge.

It furthers the University's mission by disseminating knowledge in the pursuit of education, learning, and research at the highest international levels of excellence.

www.cambridge.org
Information on this title: www.cambridge.org/9781009011808
DOI: 10.1017/9781009026840

© Susan Meld Shell 2022

First published 2022

A catalogue record for this publication is available from the British Library.

ISBN 978-1-009-01180-8 Paperback
ISSN 2397-9461 (online)
ISSN 2514-3824 (print)

The Politics Of Beauty

A Study Of Kant's Critique Of Taste

Elements in the Philosophy of Immanuel Kant

DOI: 10.1017/9781009026840
First published online: August 2022

Susan Meld Shell
Boston College
Author for correspondence: Susan Meld Shell, shell@bc.edu

Abstract: This Element examines the entirety of Kant's Critique of Taste (in Part One of the *Critique of Judgment*) with particular emphasis on its political and moral aims. Kant's critical treatment of aesthetic judgment is both an extended theoretical response to influential predecessors and contemporaries, including Rousseau and Herder, and a practical intervention in its own right meant to nudge history forward at a time of civilizational crisis. Attention to these themes helps resolve a number of puzzles, both textual and philosophic, including the normative force and meaning of judgments of taste and the relation between natural and artful beauty.

Keywords: Kant, beauty, aesthetics, politics, culture

ISBNs: 9781009011808 (PB), 9781009026840 (OC)
ISSNs: 2397-9461 (online), 2514-3824 (print)

Contents

1 Introduction: Reflection and Revolution

Although the relation between politics and aesthetics is a subject of perennial interest, the political implications of Kant's Critique of Taste (in Part One of the *Critique of Judgment*) have not previously been the focus of a sustained study. That omission is all the more striking given Kant's attention to the issue, from the 1760s onward, in response to Rousseau's famous charge that progress in the arts and sciences was inimical to moral health and collective human happiness. Kant's Critique of Taste, as I here argue, represents his definitive response to Rousseau's challenge. I do not mean to claim that this is *all* that Kant's Critique aims to accomplish; nor do I claim to offer a comprehensive account of his theory of taste. Still, a concentration on this neglected theme has two distinct advantages: *first*, it enables one to better locate Kant's aesthetic work within the larger political program he laid out in the years following the French Revolution, from the *Critique of Judgment* (1790) to the later *Metaphysics of Morals* (1798). *Second*, it brings new clarity to two much-contested interpretive issues: namely, *the relation between aesthetic judgments of natural and artistic beauty* and the *normative force and significance of aesthetic judgment as such*.

Despite the profusion of insightful scholarly work on Kant's aesthetics and politics, little has been written on their interrelation. The dramatic exception that proves the rule is Hannah Arendt, whose *Lectures on Kant's Political Philosophy* replaces his most overtly "political" philosophic work, namely, the *Doctrine of Right* (which she dismisses as a product of senility), with his critique of aesthetic judgment, which she tends to read as the political work that Kant would or should have written (Arendt, 1992). To be sure, there are obvious practical implications of Kant's aesthetic theory to which he himself explicitly points, and that have been duly noted in the literature. These include, but are not limited to, the "discipline" of weaning us from our dependence on crudely sensual pleasure and making our natural drive to sociability more decorous and "civilized," with implications for political life that are seemingly obvious. At the same time, the precise relation between Kant's aesthetics and his practical philosophy more generally is one of the outstanding unsettled scholarly issues currently being debated, with some claiming that the normative basis of Kantian aesthetics is ultimately moral and others treating such concerns as incidental to Kant's central argument.

In conflating, in defiance of Kant's own text, the "common sense" of aesthetic judgment with one directly pertinent to politics, Arendt (1992:64–72) may have been responding to Walter Benjamin's famous juxtaposition of fascism, understood as the aestheticization of politics, and communism understood as the politicization of aesthetics. As he writes at the end of "Art in the Age of Its Technical Reproducibility": "'Fiat ars – pereat mundus', says Fascism, and, as Marinetti admits, expects war to supply the artistic gratification of a sense perception that has been changed by technology .... This is the situation of politics which Fascism is rendering aesthetic. Communism responds by politicizing art" (Benjamin, 1968:242). Arendt had good reason to seek a more moderate, republican alternative to these two horns, and evidently thought she had found it in the unwritten Kantian text she attempted to compose. But there are alternative political lessons to be drawn from Kant's Critique of Taste that are both truer to Kant's meaning and ultimately more compelling, as I will argue, than those drawn either by Arendt or by some later, more textually faithful scholars.[1]

The sections that make up this study aim to chart the political conse-quences Kant hoped would flow from a critical doctrine of taste. (I mainly exclude Kant's treatment of the sublime, on whose political implications much has indeed been written, which is only indirectly the object of judg-ments of "taste" – e.g., in "beautiful" representations of the sublime.) Section 2 ("The Elements of Beauty" [*CJ* #1–40]) takes up the earliest and most commonly studied sections of the Critique of Taste, including both the "deduction" of taste at #38 and Kant's discussion of our "empirical" and "moral" interests in the beautiful. Sections 3 and 4 ("Artistic Beauty" [*CJ* #41–52] and "Rhetoric and the Antinomy of Taste" [*CJ* #53–57]) consider Kant's treatment of fine art in greater detail. Rather than either downplay these sections (like Guyer in his earlier work) or make it the central focus of Kant's doctrine of taste (like Crawford), I argue that judgments of artistic beauty make a distinctive normative claim, requiring its own independent "deduction," and that such taste (unlike a taste for free beauties of nature) develops only under specific social conditions. As such, judgments of artistic beauty have a normative character that is distinctly their own (and hence not exhausted by Kant's earlier deduction of pure judgments of natural beauty). Section 5 ("The Politics of Beauty" [*CJ* #58– 60]) discusses the final sections of the Critique of Taste, including both beauty as "symbol" and the peculiar relation, as it seems to Kant during the early months of the French Revolution, between taste and the solution to the problem of establishing a state.

In sum: this is mainly a study of Part One of the *Critique of Judgment* (minus Kant's treatment of the sublime). Unlike other such studies, mine especially focuses on what Kant aimed to accomplish practically and politically through

---

[1] For instructive suggestions, however, see Clewis (2009), Dobe (2018), and Stoner (2019).

such a critique (insofar as this can be established on the basis of the text itself). Moreover, unlike many who have touched on the latter topic,[2] I try to take seriously the moral and political harms, as well as benefits, that flow from the advance of civilization and culture. So understood, Kant's Critique of Taste, as I will argue, is itself a practical/political intervention meant to redirect taste in a more positive civil and moral direction. I do not claim this to be the primary aim of the Critique of Taste; nor is what follows intended as a comprehensive study of Kant's account of beauty. Still, as I hope to show, viewing the Critique of Taste through such a lens not only reveals a degree of *comprehensive philosophic rigor and coherence* not otherwise easily appreciated; it also suggests that Kant's Critique of Taste may harbor untapped resources for understanding and improving our own civic and aesthetic culture.[3]

This study is also distinguished from many others[4] in claiming that the normative standard of taste may be *either* constitutive *or* regulative, depending on whether natural or artistic beauty is mainly at issue. The *constitutive* standard applies to "pure judgments of taste" that presuppose a capacity shared by all human beings capable of making objective epistemic judgments. The *regulative* standard, by way of contrast, mainly applies, as I will argue, to a taste for exemplary works of art. Unlike the capacity for and exercise of pure judgments of natural beauty, the latter sort of taste must be *cultivated*, a process that is partly dependent on the progress of civilization and that gives rise to an "antinomy" that must be critically resolved if taste is to realize, rather than frustrate, its morally preparatory mission. Moreover, unlike pure judgments of taste for free beauties (of nature), which only concern the free play of imagination and understanding, taste in the regulative sense crucially involves reason as well.[5] It also presupposes a "creative" expansion of the imagination (beyond that involved in pure judgments of taste) that gives rise to both new opportunities for spiritual enlivening (e.g., through the art of poetry) and new dangers (e.g., through the misuse of rhetoric to beguile rather than elevate).

---

[2] For example, Sweet (2013), Murray (2015); but compare Kalar (2017) and Otabi (2018).

[3] Consider in this regard both Clement Greenberg's championing of abstract expressionism on putatively (and falsely) "Kantian" grounds, and Arthur Danto's counter-championing of "conceptualism" on grounds that were more Kantian than he himself evidently recognized. On these and other misappropriations of Kant's aesthetics within the contemporary art world, see Cazeaux (2021), Guyer (2021), and Costello (2007).

[4] "Regulative" readings include, for example, Crawford (1974), Longuenesse (2006), and Matherne (2019). For some alternative combined readings see Saville (1987), Kemal (1992), and Dobe (2010). According to Guyer (1979:327) and Stoner (2019) Kant leaves the matter unsettled.

[5] The significance of this addition (and hence an essential difference between the two sorts of aesthetic judgment) tends to be overlooked; an exception is Crowther (2010:142) who neglects, however, the continuing importance of the relation between imagination and understanding (as well as reason) in judgments of fine art.

The sections that follow take their initial bearings from the oft noted but insufficiently pondered coincidence of the Storming of the Bastille in July 1789 – along with its immediate political context and aftermath – and the months in which Kant completed the *Critique of Judgment*, installments of which he sent off to the printer between January and March 1790. As John Zammito (1992) has convincingly argued, building on the earlier work of Giorgio Tonelli (1966), much of the latter sections of Part One, as well as the bulk of Part Two, were written after May 1789 and some, including the final version of the "Dialectic of Aesthetic Judgment" and a greatly expanded concluding section of Part Two, were not completed until early 1790. By May 1789, much had already happened in France, including the publication of Abbé Sieyès' influential pamphlet *What Is the Third Estate?* in January of that year, followed by the king's call for elections of delegates to the Estates-General (which had not met for over a century) and the Paris riots in April; May and June witnessed the meeting of the Estates-General followed by its trans-formation, under the self-declared authority of the Third Estate, into a National Assembly which Louis XVI officially recognized in late June. Formal adoption by the Assembly of the Declaration of the Rights of Man and of the Citizen would follow in August. By December 1789, the Assembly had appropriated the property of the Church for the nation's use, introduced the assignat (a form of currency based on the value of confiscated Church property), and opened up public office to Protestants.

Kant's avid interest in revolutionary developments in France is common knowledge. According to one contemporary report, he was so caught up that he "would have walked for miles to get the mail" (Kuehn, 2001:343); and he would later admit, in an unpublished draft, to a "feverish" enthusiasm for the latest news (*Refl-E* 19:604). That Kant had events in France firmly in mind as he completed Part Two of the *Critique of Judgment* is strongly suggested by his reference, in a striking footnote, to the recent transformation of a great people into a state "organized" along republican lines, and copying almost verbatim the words of the Abbé, who writes in *What Is the Third Estate?* of the constitutional laws that can emanate from the will of a nation as of two kinds, some "determin[ing] the organization and the functions of the legislative body; the others … the organization and functions of the various executive bodies" (Sieyès, 2002:53). It seems likely, then, as Zammito (1992:334) argues, that the French Revolution contributed to a general reorientation in Kant's historical, political, and religious thinking to which the third *Critique* bears signal witness.

In Part One of the *Critique of Judgment*, the evidence is admittedly less conclusive and more subtle, as we shall see. But, in any case, the political dimensions of Kant's Critique of Taste were not limited to, or bounded by, current events but ultimately reflect deeper philosophic issues, including those raised by Rousseau as to the very possibility of genuine human progress (Allison, 2001:206). As Kant had himself stated in the *Idea for a Universal History* (1784), "we are *cultured* to a high degree through art and science. We are *civilized* – perhaps too much for our own good – in all sorts of social grace and decorum. But as to our being *moralized* – for that, much is lacking" (*IUH* 8:260). Kant's early answer to that question had suggested two possible solutions: a republic dependent on social habits of frugality and civic virtue, and a monarchic state suitable for luxurious societies (*Rem* 2:166),[6] such as contemporary Prussia, in which progress in the arts and sciences could flourish without damage to civil unity thanks to the iron rule of "enlightened" monarchs like Frederick II in the short run, and with further civil freedom left to the indefinite future (*WIE* 8:41–42). Contemporary events in France collapsed that time frame, suggesting the possibility of combining progress, stability, and republican freedom in the here and now. Indeed, as he finished the last pages of the *Critique of Judgment*, Kant would have had good reason to hope that a new constitutional monarchy with strongly republican features, and hence favorable to both intellectual and moral advancement, was then in the making, thanks to the domination in the National Assembly of moderates like Sieyès. Such hopes would have been further supported by the reports of sympathetic observers like Count Windisch-Graetz, in whose recent work on "organism" Kant took particular interest at this time (Shell, 2009:164–67).

But there were other philosophic issues at stake – not least, both the precise status of teleological principles in the conduct of natural scientific inquiry, as treated in his 1787 essay, and the very possibility of an a priori principle of taste (a possibility that he had explicitly denied in the *Critique of Pure Reason*), leading to the need for a transcendental "critique of taste." By 1787 the two questions had merged under the general rubric of the "Critique of Judgment" thanks to an expanded understanding of the scope of "reflecting," as distinguished from "determining," judgment.

That the provenance of this new a priori principle was by his own account aesthetic (*Corr* 10:513–15) adds weight to the suspicion of an important link between Kant's treatment of aesthetic judgment in the third *Critique* and his new approach to history as worldly realization, if only by continual approximation, of a highest good earlier presented as an otherworldly transcendental ideal. For, if in Kant's *Idea for Universal History* culture and civilization had proceeded, in that order, a moralization that remained problematic, now culture, issuing from mere "civilization" and infused under the title of "discipline" with

---

[6] See also Shell and Velkley (2012).

new moral promise, was pointed toward the future. That promise, to be sure, was double-edged, art never altogether losing its morally destructive association with the twin vices of vanity and luxury and giving Kant's treatment of aesthetic judgment an open-endedness particularly pertinent to our own age. What Kant foresaw was the possibility and need for a new national art suitable for the republican constitutional state that his political writings of the 1790s helped conjure forth. Part One of the *Critique of Judgment* presents the faint but distinctive outlines of that aesthetic–political project.

2 The Elements of Beauty

In #1–42 of Part One of the *Critique of Judgment*, Kant presents, in consecutive order: elucidations (*Erklärungen*) of the four "moments" (*Momenta*) of taste and beauty; a "deduction" of pure judgments of taste with regard to free beauties of nature; and, finally, a provisional inquiry into the possibility of a principle that might guide or otherwise apply to judgments of artistic beauty – aesthetic judgments of a sort that the deduction provided in #38 specifically omits. In so claiming, I take seriously Kant's promise, at the end of #20, to resolve the question of whether the "indeterminate norm" of taste is "constitutive" or "regulative" – that is, whether taste is an "original and natural faculty" or one that is "artificial" and "yet to be acquired." For as I will argue (and as the text bears out), the indeterminate norm of taste – that is, "[the idea of] common sense" – is *both constitutive* (with respect to judgments of free natural beauties) *and regulative* (with respect to judgments of artistic beauty as well as natural beauty insofar as it arouses "aesthetic ideas"). That characterization not only resolves a number of stubborn textual puzzles; it also proves peculiarly well suited to a "humanity" (*Menschheit*) whose *Anlagen* can develop fully "only in the species" (*IUH* 8:18) – a species, that is to say, whose faculty of taste is both original and natural *and* open to cultivation. The norm of taste is constitutive with respect to free beauties of nature, from which even "savages"[7] and young children can derive pure aesthetic pleasure (*CJ* 5:205 n.); while the norm of taste is regulative with respect to artistic works, which presuppose a certain degree of social sophistication in both the artist and the judge. And yet the relation of artful beauty to true human progress is "ambiguous," giving rise, as I will claim, to the need for "transcendental critique," that is, for the "science" of taste that is laid out in Parts One and Two of the Critique of Taste (the Analytic and the Dialectic, respectively). In short, Kant's Critique of Taste presents a continuous

---

[7] Although someone "abandoned on some remote island" would not bother to decorate his person or his house (*CJ* 5:297), Kant never says that human beings at the rudest stage (who are, on his account, at least minimally social) wouldn't take disinterested pleasure in the beautiful (see, e.g., *CB* 8:113). Compare Otabe (2018).

argument that not only helps to satisfy the architectonic need for a "bridge" between the realms of nature and freedom; it also represents a direct effort on Kant's part to intervene pragmatically and politically at a particularly precarious civilizational moment.

2.1 The Four "Moments" of Taste

This double aim (simultaneously theoretical and practical) is reflected in Kant's initial analysis of the "moments" of taste, which, in Kemal's (1992:29) words, begins by "looking at our ordinary way of talking about and responding to beautiful objects." In calling these conceptual elements "moments" (*Momenta*) Kant calls attention to their criterial function as "grounds" that "determine" judgments of taste.[8] In the course of explicating these determining criteria, which are always already at work in our judgments of taste, if only implicitly, he not only makes our concepts of taste more theoretically precise; he also encourages readers to become more careful and discriminating in their own aesthetic responses. The person who is made explicitly aware of the difference between, say, the pleasures of beauty and those associated with mere charm is less likely to confuse them. Kant's analysis is thus not only a theoretical exercise in conceptual description; it is also a practical contribution to what he calls the "cultivation" of taste.

The "moments" of taste are, one could say, the four-fold considerations that implicitly determine our judgments of taste, just as the four concepts that head the Table of Categories in the first *Critique* – that is, quantity, quality, relation, and modality – determine all our empirical cognitive judgments whether or not we are always aware of it consciously. In adopting those a priori "logical forms" as his guide, Kant also adapts them to his present purpose, beginning not with "quantity" (as in the first *Critique*) but instead with what in appreciating the beautiful we "notice first" – namely, "quality," that is, a subjective state consisting in a peculiar feeling of pleasure. The other moments follow in order of deepening foundational primacy (or *Gründlichkeit*), as I will argue in what follows; and they culminate in the criterion of "necessity" (under the heading "modality"). And yet unlike the earlier criteria, this final moment is not referred to (as in the earlier cases) as a "determining ground" of judgment but assimilated, instead, with an "indeterminate" norm whose precise character and force is left unresolved. For whether that norm should be understood as "constitutive" or as merely "regulative" cannot be settled, as we shall see, on the basis of the Analytic alone.

---

[8] According to Grimm and Grimm (1854), "moment" (from the Latin *momentum*) bore the contemporary meaning of "motive, or essentially deciding circumstance." See also Wenzel (2005:13–14).

Another factor bears mentioning before entering into Kant's analysis directly: namely, the social character of the aesthetic experience, and related civilizational context, that Kant here presupposes. In explicating the various moments of taste he repeatedly appeals not only to internal experience – to what one feels or is conscious of in inner sense – but also to what we commonly proclaim to one another. There may indeed be a rudimentary sort of taste that is available to isolated "savages" or young children (*CJ* 5:203 n.); but taste insofar as it presents itself most readily to critical analysis is always also oriented toward communication with others. Indeed, taste's elements would seem to make themselves fully available for deliberate reflection only where civilization is relatively advanced; whereas among those whose taste remains "barbarous," the difference between pleasures of beauty and those merely of charm may hardly be noticed let alone attentively considered (*CJ* 5:223).

The *qualitative* criterion that determines judgments of the beautiful is one of mere subjectivity. "In order to decide whether something is beautiful," we do not relate our representation to the object but to the subject and our own feeling of pleasure or displeasure (*CJ* 5:203). I do not first attend to its defining features as an object of a certain kind, but whether (and how) it pleases me. In adopting the logical forms of judgment as a template, Kant also changes their order, beginning not with "quantity" but "quality," because, as he puts it, "aesthetic judgment on the beautiful regards it first" (*CJ* 5:203 n.).

Kant's opening bears instructive comparison in this respect with Plato's *Greater Hippias*, a locus classicus of philosophic treatments of beauty, which begins with the question "what is beauty?" and ends, aporetically, after defining it as a specific sort of pleasure: namely, that associated with sight and hearing.[9] Kant begins, one could say, where Plato ends: by defining beauty as a kind of pleasure (that will indeed prove to be associated with sight and hearing), while also denying, contra Plato, that judgments of taste, as merely subjective and hence not dependent on a concept of what the object "is" or "is to be," are cognitive judgments at all. What mainly distinguishes the pleasure in the beautiful, however, is what Kant famously calls its "disinterestedness." Unlike the two other sorts of satisfaction (that engage the sensible and intellectual faculties respectively), pleasure in the beautiful has no immediate relation to the faculty of desire, and hence involves no interest in the existence of the object, be it a well-cooked meal or a virtuous will. Judgments of taste are not determined by any concept: either one pertaining to an object of cognition, or one pertaining to an object of desire.

---

9 Plato. *Greater Hippias*, 297e.

In his initial grounding of judgments of taste in a disinterested feeling of pleasure independent of any concept, Kant not only takes for granted the validity of cognitive and volitional theories that he developed in his two earlier Critiques; he also appeals by way of confirmation to common social experience: for example, general distrust of judgments of taste "in which there is mixed any interest." When a mother praises the beauty of her own child we are not inclined to take her appraisal seriously as a pure aesthetic judgment. And yet interest is also something from which we assume people can abstract for purposes of judging aesthetically: as with someone who puts his Rousseauesque indignation aside to admire a castle for its beauty.[10]

In beginning with what one "first regards" Kant speaks not only to "philosophers," then, but also in terms that are comprehensible to a broader cultivated audience: Meeting its members where they are, he will proceed to explicate, through critical analysis, the further criteria, or determining grounds, that are implicitly at work in judgments that we (members of such an audience) take ourselves to make routinely.

In turning to the second moment (under the heading of *quantity*), Kant starts with what can "be deduced [*gefolgert werden*]" from consideration of the first: namely, that the beautiful is "that which, without concepts," is represented as the object of "a *universal* satisfaction." This second criterion – that is, judgment as the representation of something as a source of universal satisfaction – follows, as Kant here claims, as a necessary consequence of the abstraction from all interest that is at least implicitly assumed in all judgments of taste. For since the accompanying pleasure is not limited by any private interest or desire that could be idiosyncratic or peculiar to the individual, it must be represented as capable of also being felt by others. Put differently, in exercising judgment of this sort, one must "believe oneself to have grounds for expecting it of everyone" (*CJ* 5:211).

Kant thus moves from what is first for us (namely, a certain pleasure in the beautiful) to what that pleasure implies but of which we may not be fully aware until it is brought to our attention: for example, by social circumstances that bring out the difference between merely private pleasures and feeling that is not only subjective but also represented as universal. Thus, as Kant goes on to note, whereas in matters of merely private pleasure (e.g., in a certain sort of wine) we are content to let others go their own way, in matters of taste as such we make a "rightful claim to the assent of everyone" and even "rebuke" (*tadeln*) those who disagree (*CJ* 5:213). Nor is there any "conflict" (*Streit*) over whether such

---

[10] See also Trullinger (2015).

claims are possible, but only over whether they are made correctly in a given case (*CJ* 5:214).

In this expectation of universal consent, one necessarily "postulates," as the condition of its possibility, that one judges with a "universal voice," though without the mediation of concepts. To be sure, that universal voice is only an "idea," the investigation of whose ground Kant here postpones. As to whether one in fact judges, in a given case, in accordance with that idea no one can be certain. But that one believes oneself to do so can be deduced from the mere fact that one judges something to be beautiful (*CJ* 5:216).

This brings Kant to a crucial question that he calls the "key to the critique of taste": namely, which comes first, pleasure or the judging of the object? And it might well seem, since pleasure is not only what we notice first, but also what determines judgments of taste under the heading of quality, that it was also first in order of *Gründlichkeit*. But in fact, as we have already seen, judgments of taste must also be determined, under the heading of quantity, by a universality that presupposes the idea of a universal voice. And in any case, were pleasure to come first in a more ultimate sense, we would be incapable of distinguishing pleasure in the beautiful from other subjective pleasures associated with the merely agreeable. For in that case, the pleasure would "immediately depend on the representation through which the object *is given*" (*CJ* 5:217). Hence the criterion of universal communicability must precede that of disinterested pleasure as a determining ground of our judgment (even though we may not always be consciously aware of the former's necessary precedence).

And since only that which is associated in some way with cognition is universally communicable, and judgments of taste abstract from any concept of an object, the state of mind in question must itself be one of free play, or mutual harmony, independent of any concept, of the forces of cognition – that is, one involving the "proportioned disposition" (*proportionirte Stimmung*) that everyone requires for all cognition (*CJ* 5:519). The difference in the case of beauty is that this disposition arises "freely," rather than, as with ordinary cognition, through imagination's constrained conformity to rules of the understanding.[11]

In sum: If in judgments of taste disinterested pleasure is the criterion or determining ground that we notice *first*, it proves, on further consideration, to necessarily imply a *second*: namely, subjective universality, along with the accompanying postulation of an idea of a universal voice as condition of the latter's possibility. But such a universal voice is itself possible, in turn, only if our pleasure "represents" a state of mutual enlivening harmony between

---

[11] This consideration would seem to meet the frequently raised objection that were Kant's account to hold, *all* objects of cognition would have to be judged beautiful.

imagination and understanding – that is to say, a "proportionate disposition" on their part that insofar as it is particularly apt for cognition generally is also, as such, universally sharable (*CJ* 5:219).[12]

This final consideration is gateway to a *third* criterion, under the heading of *relation*, which relates the purposiveness of that proportional disposition (purposive, that is to say, for cognition generally) and the merely formal purposiveness that characterizes the object (or its representation) that is judged to be beautiful – a purposiveness that thereby reveals its own "purposiveness of form." "Purposiveness," speaking "transcendentally," is the "*causality*" of a concept with regard to its *object*" (*CJ* 5:220). Purposiveness names, in other words, the relation between an object (e.g., a chair) and the concept (e.g., the carpenter's plan) that makes it "real[ly] possible." We can explain the existence of a chair only by appealing to the concept of a chair as its final cause. But purposiveness can exist "even without an end," so long as we can explain the existence of an object in no other way; and we can observe such purposiveness of form, even without an end, albeit only by reflection (e.g., in our observation of animals and other natural ends) (*CJ* 5:220).

It is purposiveness of the latter sort that furnishes a third "determining ground" of judgments of taste (*CJ* 5:221). In this case, however, no end at all is taken into account – neither the *subjective* end, which would make interest the ground of satisfaction, nor the *objective* end to which reflective judgment of natural ends itself appeals. But judgment of an object as beautiful is accompanied, as Kant has shown, by a pleasure that is declared to be universally valid through that very judgment. Hence, nothing remains to count, under the heading of relation, as its determining ground other than the "subjective purposiveness in the representation of an object without any end," be it subjective or objective. But this means that "the mere form of purposiveness in the representation through which the object is *given* to us" – at least "insofar as we are conscious of it" – can constitute the pleasure that we judge, without a concept, to be

---

[12] This reading has the advantage of eliminating the seeming contradiction involved in Kant claiming *both* that judging "comes first" (*CJ* 5:217) and that the pleasure is itself a determining ground of judgment (e.g., at *CJ* 5:204). It is largely to avoid this difficulty that Crawford (1974) and Guyer (1979), among others, have argued that judgments of taste proceed in two stages: the first, determined by the play of cognitive faculties; the second, involving reflection on the accompanying pleasure and its communicability. My account differs from most "one-stage" theories (e.g., Ginsborg [1991], Zuckert [2007]) inasmuch as I distinguish between judgments of taste in their most rudimentary form and after taste has been "cultivated" (e.g., through the sort of education Kant is here providing). In the later, cultivated case, the act of judgment, along with its several moments, becomes an object of reflection in its own right. On my reading, this reflection is an intentional continuation and drawing out of the first rather than a separate act of judgment in its own right. For an analogous drawing out of a cognitive faculty's implicit principle, see *G* 4:404. (My thanks to Samuel Stoner for this point.)

universally communicable, and thereby also constitute the judgment of taste's "determining ground."

To the earlier criteria or "determining grounds" of judgments of taste Kant has now added a third, implicit in the two preceding it. Order of presentation (and discovery) thus reverses the order of conceptual priority, with each moment presupposing the one that follows, as is revealed by the stages of critically guided reflection through which Kant draws the reader. There is thus no need to choose between the two-stage theories that posit two acts of aesthetic judgment and one-stage theories that posit a single judgment of complex self-reflection. For the criterion of such judgments that first comes to notice, and is most salient to the beginner, is supplemented and deepened, on further conscious reflection, by grounds that are already present but whose explication can make our judgments of taste both sharper and more subtle. Thus, as Kant here puts it, the person "of still barbarous taste," who is barely able to distinguish the pleasures of the beautiful from those of mere charm and emotion, can become more discriminating "through careful determination of these concepts" (*CJ* 5:223). By this I take Kant to mean that whereas all three "moments" or criteria are implicitly at work in our judgments of the beautiful, we are likely to become explicitly aware of them as such only on the basis of conscious reflection and analysis – a process that can in turn make taste less barbarous and more careful. There is thus no contradiction at work (as is sometimes held) in Kant's claiming, on the one hand, that pleasure is the determining ground of judgments of the beautiful, and his also claiming, on the other, that this pleasure presupposes further determining grounds – that our pleasure in the beautiful "represents," and of which it is itself, as he also puts it, the conscious "effect" (*CJ* 5:221).

In sum: Judgments of taste in their initial and most primitive form are determined by all four moments or criteria, just as the cognitive judgments that Kant draws on as a model are determined by the categories under the headings of Quantity, Quality, Relation, and Modality. In both cases, such judgment happens for the most part subconsciously, though one can be made more fully aware of its determining elements through intentional reflection and analysis. In aesthetic judgment of the beautiful, such *intentional* reflection not only has theoretical significance; it also contributes, I would suggest, to what Kant calls "practicing" and "cultivating" one's taste.

But with philosophic refinement also come errors, such as those committed by "philosophers of repute" who assimilate judgments of taste to "confused" judgments of perfection. It is thus of the "greatest importance," as Kant puts it (*CJ* 5:227), to decide whether beauty is indeed reducible to a concept of perfection, albeit one thought only confusedly, as many distinguished thinkers affirm. To be sure, as Kant has previously shown, our judgments of the beautiful do not depend on and/or specifically abstract from any concept of what the object "is to be," so ruling out dependence on any concept of perfection, be it external or internal. Neither the end the object is to serve, nor its completeness as a member of a certain kind, nor the concept that supplies the rule for its internal unity here applies. For what is merely "formal" in an object's representation does not allow "any cognition of objective purposiveness at all," leaving nothing but the "subjective purposiveness of the representation in the mind of the beholder."[13]

And yet more is evidently needed if the refutation of perfectionism is to be compelling: namely, attention to a further feature of the "free play" of the forces of cognition – a feature that is "indicated" by this "subjective purposiveness" and consisting in a certain "ease" (*Behaglichkeit*) of apprehension,[14] not earlier mentioned, on the part of the imagination (*CJ* 5:227). In contrast to the apprehension of a preliminary schema on imagination's part that occurs in cases of cognition, in cases of the beautiful imagination instead apprehends a form (or schema) that harmonizes with the understanding spontaneously, as it were, and without being guided, in an anticipatory fashion, by the rules of the understanding that would otherwise be needed. Indeed, it is just this "ease," that distinguishes, as its "*specific* difference" (*CJ* 5:228), the subjective harmony that grounds aesthetic judgment from the harmony that applies in ordinary cases of cognition in which imagination finds itself constrained by foreign rules.

This ease is not only a specific marker of judgments of the beautiful, providing a ready, subjectively available means for distinguishing them from judgments of perfection; it also explains why we "linger over the beautiful" – not through an *external* causality as with objects that have "charm" over which we also "linger,"[15] but rather through an "internal causality" or "causality in itself" not only to maintain oneself in one's present state (as with any pleasure) but to do so indefinitely (*CJ* 5:222). Pleasure in the beautiful thus has a certain tireless quality, unlike agreeable pleasures that soon fade and become boring unless reinforced externally, for example, through novelty and variety (*CJ* 5:243). For in the latter case the mind remains "passive"; whereas "consideration of the beautiful" is "self-reproduc[ing]" and "self-strengthen[ing]" (*CJ* 5:222).[16]

We will have reason to return to this subject when we take up exemplary works of art in Section 3 ("Artistic beauty"), which exhibit their own peculiar sort of "perfection." For the present it suffices to note that the mental activity involved in "pure" judgments of taste is neither cognitive nor practical (both of which would require a concept of what the object is to be) but self-maintaining

---

[13] As Guyer (1997) observes, this does not rule out, especially in the case of judgments of fine art, the *presence* of concepts.

[14] See also Allison (2001:75).   [15] Compare Zuckert (2007).   [16] Compare Lehman (2018).

on its own. Pleasure in the beautiful, so considered, not only *is*, as Kant here puts it, our consciousness of the free play of the mind in its formal purposiveness; it also "contains a determining ground of the activity of the subject" with regard to that mutual animation (*CJ* 5:222). Like any sensual satisfaction, pleasure in the beautiful "causes" one to remain in one's present state; and yet unlike ordinary pleasures that signal the promotion of the vital forces that we share with other animals, the pleasure in the beautiful not only enables us to feel, but also itself actively promotes, living forces of a higher order (cf. *CPrR* 5:162). Pleasure in the beautiful both "represents" or signals *mental* life activity and tends subsequently to sustain it.

This consideration clarifies Kant's earlier flat rejection (as it may have seemed), at the beginning of *Critique of Judgment* #9, of the claim that with regard to the beautiful, "pleasure comes before the judgment," despite his own apparent statements to the contrary elsewhere. Kant had rested that rejection on the fact that were pleasure to come first, it would be indistinguishable from satisfaction in the agreeable, "since it would immediately depend on the representation through which the object *is given*" (*CJ* 5:217). But as he has now drawn out in explicating moment three, pleasure can be causal without immediately depending on representation of the object "as given," that is, as in cases of ordinary cognition. For in the case at hand, it is not "the representation through which the object is *given* to us," but the "purposiveness" of this representation "insofar as we are conscious of it" that is judged "universally communicable" (*CJ* 5:221). In short, that judgment can and must "go first" does not negate the causal role of pleasure in arousing and maintaining the activity of which it is also the "effect." And it is thus unsurprising that pleasure is what we tend to *notice* first, since it is our lingering, without the need for constantly renewed external prompts, that is likely to first draw our attention to what makes taste distinctive.

But Kant has an additional consideration in mind: "pure" judgments of taste are not only distinguished from those that are influenced by charm and emotion, but also from judgments concerning what he calls "adherent" or "dependent" beauty.[17] For here judgment must meet the prior condition of satisfying a standard of perfection that is itself based on a concept of what the object in question is "to be" or is otherwise good for (*CJ* 5:229). This perfection can be either external (as with, e.g., a church) or internal, and in the latter case, related either to a natural end (e.g., a horse) or to an end in itself (e.g., a human being qua rational being). Thus a horse cannot be called beautiful, however otherwise

---

[17] On Kant's evolving understanding of the distinction between pure and adherent beauty, see Clewis (2018).

pleasing its shape, if it lacks legs. And a church, however graceful its design, cannot be called beautiful if it is unsuitable for purposes of worship.

In its dependence on an aesthetically extraneous standard of perfection, adherent beauty raises particularly interesting questions that bear directly on the status of the sort of artistic beauty that Kant later calls "exemplary," but that is not here pursued.[18] And indeed, fine art proves to require a specific sort of aesthetic norm that Kant will take up in his treatment of works of genius – works that are free, as we shall see, of the "dependence on a determinate concept" by which imagination, in judgments of adherent beauties such as horses and churches, is normally "restricted" (*CJ* 5:230).

In anticipation of that later treatment Kant here provides a curious and somewhat perplexing addition – an "ideal of beauty" that applies solely to the human being, especially "*the human figure*" (*der menschlichen Gestalt*), and for which a certain cultivation of taste, beyond that required in pure judgments of taste thus far described, is evidently necessary. First, it is unclear whether Kant means by such an object of ideal beauty a living human being (i.e., a "beauty of nature") or the latter's artful portrayal in painting or sculpture. Indeed, it would seem that an actual human being who could represent such an ideal would always already also be a product of artful self-presentation reflective of the particularities of climate and custom (*CJ* 5:234–35). But if the latter is the case, then Kant's otherwise strict dichotomy between natural and artful beauty may not here apply.[19]

Second, it is likewise unclear whether the term "adherent" properly applies to the "ideal of beauty," despite its evident dependence on a concept of what the object is to be. (And, indeed, that term will not appear in Kant's later treatment of exemplary works of art). For while aesthetic judgment of ideal beauty is evidently not "pure," it also makes demands that go beyond what is required for other judgments of beauty, be they dependent or free: namely, a union of "ideas of reason" with "great might of imagination" – a union that is itself a product of human freedom (*CJ* 5:232) and that is required, as Kant specifically notes, not only in one who would "present" ideal beauty but also in one "who would merely judge [it]" (*CJ* 5:235). Moreover, while independence from all sensory

---

[18] With the qualified exception of musical fantasias, none of the examples that Kant offers here are products of fine art as later defined. Many interpreters treat works of fine art as examples of adherent beauty; but compare Section 2 below.

[19] Compare Kant's earlier *CB* (8:113): "[Women's sexual] *refusal* was the first artifice [*Kunststück*] for leading from the merely sensed stimuli [*Reizen*] over into ideal ones [involving the productive imagination], from merely animal desire gradually over to love, and with the latter from the feeling of the merely agreeable over to the taste for beauty, in the beginning only in human beings but then, however, also in nature. Moreover, propriety [*Sittsamkeit*] . . . gave the first hint toward the formation [*Ausbildung*] of the human being as a moral creature." On the Rousseauian provenance of Kant's argument, see Shell and Velkley (2012:1–10).

charm marks that ideal as "correct," its "allowance of great interest" also proves that it is not "a mere judgment of taste" (*CJ* 5:236). And it raises the question, here left unanswered, of how judgments of ideal beauty (which are no longer, as Kant puts it, "mere" judgments of taste) exceed or otherwise differ from the merely tasteful (*CJ* 5:233).

In any case, both the presentation and the judging of beauty in accordance with its "ideal" norm presuppose a degree of cultivation, aesthetic *and* moral, that is not only uncommon but also presumably more likely to found in some societies and historical eras than others, thus posing a challenge to their universality that raises a new question as to their a priori character. For if we cannot expect others to accede to our judgments on the basis of our shared cognitive capacities alone, it is difficult to see what other a priori basis for such expectation might replace it. Kant's treatment of the ideal of beauty thus serves as a useful point of entry for considering the final moment or criterion of beauty, under the heading of *modality*, and paying particular attention to the kind of "necessitating" norm that might apply to judgments of taste.

The necessity that is "thought" in a judgment of taste is neither theoretical nor practical but both "exemplary" and "conditional." By "exemplary," Kant means that the judgment is thought of as instantiating "a universal rule," albeit that "one cannot state [*angeben*]" and that nonetheless requires others to judge similarly (*CJ* 5:237). This exemplary character distinguishes the sort of "necessity" that is peculiar to judgments of taste from that which applies to a priori cognitive and practical judgments, respectively, in which the rule is or can be made explicit. The universality in question, moreover, applies not so much to the pleasurable feeling itself (as in Kant's earlier discussion of "subjective universality") as to the "rule" that "should" determine the judgment of everyone. What Kant here means to consider, in other words, is not what can immediately be deduced from the disinterestedness of the pleasure (as in moment two), but the underlying norm that one implicitly invokes in requiring others to agree.

This necessity or "should" is, to be sure, "conditional" – first, because one cannot assume that others will subsume a given case under the rule of the example, or "compel" them to do so by objective proof (*CJ* 5:237). All one is entitled to is the "promise" that such agreement will be forthcoming. But second, that necessity is "conditional" on the "idea of a common sense" (*Gemeinsinnes*). Kant's replacement of the term "universal voice" (*allgemeine Stimme*, with its emphasis primarily on the subjective experience of the judge) with the term "common sense" (*Gemeinsinne*, as a faculty or feeling in the absence of which no norm would be universally applicable) signals a change of focus from the subjective state of mind of the one judging to the necessitating claim or expectation – that is, the "should" – thereby laid on others. "Common sense" in the sense here intended is neither an external sense, nor the common sense of Aristotle, nor the "common sense" that Kant will later invoke as a synonym for "common understanding."[20] By "common sense" Kant here means that universally communicable feeling or, alternatively, universal capacity for it, the idea of which judgments of taste presuppose (if only implicitly) in their "exemplarity."

Such a presupposition is not without a ground or reason, as Kant argues, given the universal communicability of the disposition (*Stimmung*) of the faculties that is required for empirical cognition generally. But if this is so, "that proportion which belongs to a given representation (through which an object is given to us) in order to constitute cognition," and serves as the latter's "subjective condition," must also be universally communicable. Now this disposition will presumably assume a distinct (*verschiedene*) proportion that will vary with the diversity (*Verschiedenheit*) of the objects (*CJ* 5:238). Still, there must be some proportion, not necessarily linked to this or that particular object, that is "maximally advantageous" (*zuträglichste*) for "the mutual animation of both forces of the mind," be that proportion associated with the representation of a rose, house, or something else (*CJ* 5:239). And it is just this optimality of form in one's presentation of what is given, however various the objects may be, for the mutual animating of imagination and understanding that prompts the feeling of the beautiful and that must as such be capable of prompting the same state of mind in others, that is, be universally communicable.

The "idea" of common sense that pure judgments of taste, in their exemplary necessity, presuppose is thus not merely an illusion; for, as Kant has just shown, we have "ground" (*Grund*) to assume a "common sense" (*CJ* 5:238) understood as a shared capacity to feel a state of mind in which imagination and understanding are in an accord that is optimally advantageous[21] for cognition in general. Such a state is prompted not by the representation of just *any* object, moreover, but only by those we deem beautiful, that is, those whose merely formal representation by the imagination prompts a free accord with the lawfulness of understanding – one that is unconstrained by the determinate rules that restrict imagination in the case of ordinary cognitive judgments.[22]

---

[20] Compare Arendt's conflation of the two sorts of "common sense" and accompanying assimilation of political and aesthetic judgment (1992:64, 66–69, 70–72); with *CJ* 5:294–95.

[21] On aesthetic pleasure understood as an "intensive magnitude," see Zinkin (2006).

[22] This would seem to solve the so-called "particularity" problem that has troubled many scholars who wonder why, if the disposition in question facilitates cognition in general, all objects are not judged beautiful (for a helpful treatment of this issue, see Dobe [2010]).

Kant has now established what in judgments of taste is "thought" under the heading of "modality" – namely, a "subjective necessity" that is "represented as objective under the presupposition of a common sense" (*CJ* 5:239), a presupposition, moreover, that is not ungrounded, given Kant's definition of satisfaction in the beautiful as a pleasure that is disinterested, universal, and subjective and that involves an active causality that is purposive without purpose and, as such, wholly internal.

To be sure, this "ground" cannot replace the "deduction" of the a priori principle of taste that Kant will offer in *Critique of Judgment* #38.[23] First, the argument presented in #20 rests on facts related to pleasure in the beautiful, which we can distinguish from satisfaction in the merely agreeable only empirically (and imperfectly). For all we know thus far, neither we nor others have ever actually felt the pleasure of the beautiful in its purity. Its possibility is, in this sense, thus far merely notional.

Equally crucially, "common sense" as here presented can be understood in either of two ways:[24] either as the actual communicable "effect" of the "free play" of the forces of the mind (*CJ* 5:238) or, alternatively, as a shared "capacity" (*Vermögen*) (*CJ* 5:240) for such a "feeling" (*CJ* 5:239), perhaps not yet developed.[25] Thus, although this indeterminate norm of common sense "is actually [*wirklich*] presupposed by us" whenever we make judgments of taste (as Kant's analytic treatment of its four moments concludes),

> Whether in fact [*in der That*] there is such a common sense as a constitutive principle of the possibility of experience, or whether a still higher principle of reason only makes it a regulative principle for us to bring about such a common sense in us for higher ends; thus whether taste is an original [*ursprünglich*] and natural faculty or only the idea of a faculty that is artful/artificial [*künstlich*] and still to be acquired so that a judgment of taste, with its expectation [*Zumuthung*] of universal assent, is in fact only a demand of reason [*Vernunftforderung*] to bring about such a unanimity in the way of sensing [*Sinnesart*], and the "should," i.e., the objective necessity of the confluence [*Zusammensfliessens*] of the feeling of everyone with that of each, signifies only the possibility of coming to agreement [*einträchtig*] in this, the judgment of taste only providing an example of the application of this principle – this we would not and cannot yet investigate here. (*CJ* 5:240)

To be sure, Kant had spoken in the Introduction of a promised "constitutive principle with regard to the feeling of pleasure or displeasure" (*CJ* 5:197); and yet he had not there linked such a principle, as he does here, to the "possibility of

---

[23] Compare Guyer (1979).   [24] On "common sense," see also Stoner (2019).

[25] This qualification will prove important in distinguishing between free beauties of nature and works of artful beauty – an appreciation for which partly depends on the vicissitudes of history and culture.

experience." Might taste have a "constitutive principle" of another sort? Or, alternatively, might its principle be both "constitutive" and "regulative," depending on the kind of beauty to which taste directs itself?[26] And might this explain why Kant here defines "common sense" in two different ways: both as communicable *feeling* and as merely a common *capacity* there for? Finally, in what sense, if any, might a "constitutive" norm of common sense remain, nevertheless, "only an idea"? A fuller answer to such questions cannot proceed without a transcendental "deduction" of the a priori basis of our judgments of taste.

2.2 The Deduction of Pure Aesthetic Judgments

Few issues in Kant's aesthetics are as fraught as the deduction of taste, with major disagreements not only as to Kant's underlying argument but even as to where to locate the deduction textually. It is impossible in a brief work to address such questions adequately. Still, significant progress can be made by attending more closely than is common to the fact that the "deduction" presented in *Critique of Judgment* #38 applies solely to the "beauty of things in nature" as "free beauties" (*CJ* 5:280, 279, 291),[27] leaving open the question of whether and how judgment of artful beauty (which Kant's treatment of the elements of taste had at least implicitly included) might also be critically grounded and justified.

As we shall see, Kant's answer to the latter question is complex, and will be directly addressed only in the closing sections of the Dialectic (cf. *CJ* 5:346). To anticipate: the "deduction" that is presented at #38 only concerns judgments of "free" natural beauties [*CJ* 5:280], whose justification suffices for purposes of solving the problem (*Aufgabe*) of how "a [pure] judgment of taste is possible" (*CJ* 5:288) and for thereby establishing "the a priori principle of the faculty of judgement" as such (*CJ* 5:286).[28]

---

[26] For an instructive treatment of the norm of taste as *both* constitutive and regulative, see Dobe (2010).

[27] I read the heading of #30 ("The deduction of aesthetic judgments concerning objects of nature may not be directed towards that which we call sublime among them, but only to the beautiful") as a gloss on what Kant means by "pure aesthetic judgments" for purposes of the Deduction generally – that is, judgments regarding "free beauties" that also make few if any culturally specific assumptions (as with wallpaper designs, whose "free" character might well depend on social context: what appears as a graceful curve to some might be perceived as writing by others). The references to fine art that follow (e.g., the young poet) are meant to illustrate the autonomy of taste – that is, the absence of determinate rules by which agreement might be compelled. Not counting as "pure" (in the sense earlier defined), they do not represent the sort of beauty whose principle the Deduction aims to justify. Kant makes this clear at the end of #30 by assimilating "the deduction of taste" to "[the deduction of] judgments about the beautiful things in nature" (*CJ* 5:280). Nevertheless, many critics read the Deduction as if it were meant to be adequate for *all* judgments of taste (including a taste for fine art).

[28] See Dobe (2010).

And yet, as Kant here adds, the task of the "transcendental" critic (or of criticism as "science" rather than as "art") is not exhausted by the deduction of pure judgments of taste regarding beauties of nature, but also includes resolving the question of how a judgment of taste regarding *fine art* is possible. The task of a transcendental critique of taste is not only to "develop and justify the subjective principle of taste as an a priori principle of judgment" – a problem that will presumably be solved by the deduction at #38 – but also to criticize our capacity to judge "products of fine art" (*CJ* 5:286).

We will take up the latter issue in later sections of this Element. But let us turn first to the question addressed in the "deduction" at #38: namely, how a *pure* judgment of taste is possible. That deduction, as Kant informs us, differs from his earlier discussion of the "modality" of taste by reversing the order of procedure.[29] There he had reasoned from what is first in order of ordinary discovery, beginning from the sort of pleasure that accompanies judgments of taste, and moving, through consecutive moments, to the latter's necessary positing of an idea of common sense. Here, by way of contrast, he begins by initially "abstracting" from "the feeling of pleasure" (i.e., the "content" of judgments of taste) and instead first compares its mere "form" to that of judgments of cognition (*CJ* 5:281). For, as he puts it here, the task of criticism as a science is to "derive the possibility of [judgments of taste] from the nature of [the faculty of judgment] as a faculty of cognition in general" (*CJ* 5:286).

The principle of a judgment of taste is one of subsumption, although not, as with judgments of cognition, of intuitions under concepts but rather of the faculty of imagination under the faculty of understanding – imagination, that is, in its freedom to schematize independent of concepts, and understanding in its lawfulness in general, such that their accord (unlike that afforded by cognitive judgments) is reciprocally animating (*CJ* 8:287). Thus what is "properly asserted" in a priori judgments of taste does not directly relate to the categories of the understanding. But what is asserted a priori also does not bear directly on the pleasure that accompanies this subsumption (for the judgment "I am feeling pleasure" is merely empirical). What is asserted is instead the "universal validity" of that pleasure, such that the faculty of judgment is itself, subjectively, "both object and at the same time law" (*CJ* 5:289). In short, in a pure judgment of taste, the power of judgment lays down an a priori rule for its own subsumptive act.

---

[29] Both Guyer (1997) and Allison (2001), who locate the Deduction in #22 and #38 respectively, ignore this difference in procedural order.

This brings us to the deduction proper at #38, which proceeds by showing that the a priori principle of pure judgments of taste is the same as the principle that establishes the a priori conditions of the use of the power of judgment generally. It begins with the proposition (as demonstrated earlier in the Analytic) that in a pure judgment of taste pleasure in its object is bound up with the mere judging of its form. But that form, as has been shown, is nothing other than the subjective purposiveness of its representation for judgment itself. Now, the *formal* rules of the power of judgment (i.e., rules limited neither by a particular way of sensing nor a particular concept of the understanding) must direct themselves to the conditions of the use of the power of judgment as such. Those rules can be directed only to the subjective element in judging that is necessary for cognition generally and that can thus be presupposed in all human beings. Hence, the felt purposiveness of an object we judge as beautiful is a purposiveness with respect to the subjective condition of judgments of cognition generally and can therefore "rightly be expected [*ansinnen*] in the case of everyone" (*CJ* 5:290).

In short, the a priori rules that constitute the a priori subjective condition for the use of cognitive judgment generally are also the rules, free conformity to which we sense, in judging an object of pure taste to be beautiful. But such conditions are necessarily the same for all subjects capable of communicating their objective experience (see *CJ* 5:239). Hence we are justified in holding pure judgments of taste to be valid a priori for everyone.

The "common sense" presupposed by pure judgments of taste would thus seem to be the "constitutive principle" that Kant had promised in his two Introductions (*CJ* 5:197; 20:223–24). For "common sense" as here presented would indeed seem to be an "original and natural faculty," as he had put it in #22, coeval with the capacity for (communicable) empirical cognition, rather than one that must be "acquired" (*CJ* 5:240). And yet the question he had raised there as to the character of common sense – that is, as to whether it is "original and natural" or only the idea of something still to be "acquired" – has not been fully resolved. Might the capacity to judge artful beauty presuppose a norm of the latter sort, that is, one requiring guidance by a "yet higher principle of reason" (*CJ* 5:240)?[30]

As if to provoke such a thought, Kant returns, in #40 to the topic of aesthetic "common sense," which is now explicitly contrasted with the "common sense" (in the sense of healthy common understanding) that accompanies a proper "way of thinking" generally.[31] For unlike common sense of the latter sort, which indeed characterizes *all* sound use of the cognitive faculties (5:294–95),

---

[30] For a similar suggestion along these lines, see Kalar (2017).   [31] Compare Arendt (1992).

aesthetic common sense as here (newly) "defined" is concerned not with the object "*as given* [by nature]" (*CJ* 5:219) (as in his earlier considerations of the beautiful) but with "a given representation" (*CJ* 5:295). In making this subtle change, Kant implicitly signals the expansion of taste's target to include artful beauty; for, as he will later state, whereas "a beauty of nature is a *beautiful thing*; the beauty of art is a *beautiful representation* of a thing" (*CJ* 5:311).

And to make even clearer the newly expansive meaning of "common sense" as an "indefinite" aesthetic norm, Kant now adds that his "deduction" of taste – a deduction that had only justified an "imputation" (*ansinnen*) of the universal agreement of others (*CJ* 5:290; 288) – may fall short of what is needed: namely, an account why such agreement is not just "solicited" or "imputed" but "expected" of everyone "as if it were a duty" (*CJ* 5:290). To account for the latter, and for the accompanying "demand of reason" to "produce" such a universal agreement (*CJ* 5:240), would require that we are able to assume "that the mere universal communicability of one's feeling must itself already involve an interest for us" (*CJ* 5:296), namely, in the existence of such agreement (and of works worthy of eliciting it).

2.3 Interest in the Beautiful

If such a "demand" on the part of taste is to be justified there must be an "interest," then, that is consistent with the "disinterested" character of judgments of taste as such. Kant first turns to our *"empirical" interest* in the beautiful (#41), even though such an interest, as he almost immediately concedes, is "of no importance" for the purposes at hand, namely, accounting for the claim of taste insofar as we regard it as a "demand" bordering on "duty." For the latter would instead require an interest that can be drawn "from the judgment of taste a priori, if only directly" and hence provide a clear "transition from sensory enjoyment to moral feeling" (*CJ* 5:297).

Kant begins with empirical interest nonetheless, I would suggest, in order to begin to address directly the Rousseauian challenge to which he had earlier alluded (*CJ* 5:204–5). He readily admits that there is something to Rousseau's charge:

> This much can certainly be said about the empirical interest in objects of taste and in taste itself, namely, that since the latter indulges inclination, although this may be ever so refined, it also gladly allows itself to be melted down [*zusammenschmelzen*] with all the inclinations and passions that reach their highest stage in society, and the interest in the beautiful, if so grounded, could yield only a very ambiguous transition from the agreeable to the good. (*CJ* 5:298)

To be sure, to the extent that our empirical interest in the beautiful is connected to a "sociability" belonging "to *humanity*" (*Humanität*) (*CJ* 5:297), it must have some goodly purpose:

> The beautiful interests empirically only in *society*; and if one grants that the drive toward society is natural to human beings, and the suitability and tendency toward it, i.e., *sociability*, is an exigency [*Erforderniss*] of human beings as creatures destined for society; hence as a property belonging to *humanity* [*Humanität*], then ... taste [must] also be regarded as a faculty for judging everything by means of which one can share even his *feeling* with everyone else, and hence as a means for promoting what is required [*verlangt*] by an inclination natural to everyone. (*CJ* 5:296–97)

If one grants that we are "creatures destined for society," then refinement (as "the beginning of civilization"), must play some sort of positive role, whatever Rousseau may (seem to) claim:

> only in society does it occur to [one] to be not merely a human being but also, in [one's] own way, ... refined (the beginning of civilization); for this is how we judge someone who is inclined to share his pleasure with others and is skilled at it, and who is not content with an object if he cannot feel his satisfaction with it in community with others. Moreover, each expects [*erwartet*] and demands [*fordert*] of everyone else a regard for universal communication as if from an original contract dictated by humanity [*Menschheit*] itself ; and thus at first, to be sure, only charms [*Reize*], e.g., colors for painting oneself ..., but with time also beautiful forms (as on canoes, clothing, etc) that do not in themselves provide any gratification (i.e., satisfaction of enjoyment [*Genusses*]) become important in society and combined with great interest. (*CJ* 5:297)

At long last, when "civilization ... has reached its highest point," this interest becomes "nearly the chief work of refined civilization," and sensations "are held to have value only to the extent that they allow themselves to be universally communicated." At such a point: "*even though the pleasure [Lust] that each has in ... an object is insignificant and without noticeable interest, the idea of its universal communicability increases its value almost infinitely*" (*CJ* 5:297; emphasis added).

In this anthropologically rich set of remarks, Kant traces the course of civilization from human beings' first social use of objects of charm and beauty in order to appear "refined" to others and advances to civilization's "highest point," when the mere idea of something's universal communicability raises its value "almost infinitely." In this last stage, the "idea that something is universally communicable" eclipses any actual pleasure in the beautiful and objects of taste are valued less for the disinterested pleasure they provide than because they are approved by others. The "idea of universal communicability" rather than "the idea of common *sense*," becomes the implicit norm of social taste. It is no wonder that in such a Rousseauian dystopia, in which the autonomy of taste gives way to the desire for social approval, men's empirical interest in the beautiful, based on their natural drive to society, "gladly allows itself" – along with "taste" itself – "to melt together [*Zusammenschmelzen*]" (like gold diluted by baser coin) with "inclinations and passions" at their highest level of diversity and strength (*CJ* 5:297–98).[32]

Hence empirical interest in the beautiful affords "only a very ambiguous transition" from "sensual enjoyment [*Sinnengenuss*] to moral feeling [*Sittengefühl*]" (*CJ* 5:298), and can be of little help in justifying our concept of taste as something that is not only "original and natural" (as with the taste for free beauties of nature) but must (and ought) to be "acquired" (cf. *CJ* 5:240). In short, as Kant here concludes, it is only "what can be related to judgments of taste a priori," if only indirectly, that could provide the sought for justification of reproach for those found lacking in taste.

But there is additional reason to look for such an interest; for taste would then "reveal a transition" within the faculty of judgment between the agreeable and the good that would not only provide for taste's more "purposive use"; it would also supply the "central link [*Mittelglied*]" in the "chain of human a priori faculties" (*CJ* 5:298) to which the Introduction to the *Critique of Judgment* had earlier appealed (*CJ* 5:176–77). Only interest in a "form" that is "a priori" could accomplish all these tasks. And yet "pure taste" as elaborated thus far – that is, as applying only to free beauties (of nature) as distinguished from "adherent beauties" – proves insufficient on its own.

To be sure, to take a moral interest in natural beauty habitually is a sign of moral "character," especially when a preference for natural beauty involves a sacrifice of other pleasures (*CJ* 5:298). Should someone with enough taste to judge "with the greatest correctness and refinement" prefer natural beauties that are less perfect in form to products of art that "at best yield merely social joys," even to the point of being willing to risk his or her well-being for the sake of the former's existence, it would offer a reliable indication of a mental disposition [*Gemüthstimmung*] favorable to moral feeling (*CJ* 5:299–300). Should such a person gladly depart from a room filled with artificial beauties that sustain "vanity and idleness":

---

[32] Cultivation of the capacity to take disinterested pleasure in exemplary works of art will tend, accordingly, to reverse that negative ratio, and with it a process of "idealization" that exacerbates the harms of civilization more generally. Compare Guyer (1993:256–58).

in order to find a lust [*Verlust*], as it were, for his spirit [*Geist*] in a course of thought [*Gedankengange*] that he can never develop fully: we would regard his choice with high esteem and presuppose him to have a beautiful soul, to which no knower or lover of art can claim on account of his interest in the latter. (*CJ* 5:300)

And yet this evidence would not show what is here required: namely, that an a priori interest arises from aesthetic form alone. For it was not the *form* exhibited by natural beauties (which might be inferior in form to artful beauties) that led the morally dispositioned aesthete to prefer them but the (morally encouraging) wonder they evoked that nature should be beautiful at all (*CJ* 5:300).

The extended treatment of fine art that follows is thus a necessary step forward in Kant's overall argument rather than the inconsistent or tangential digression for which it is sometimes taken.[33] For if the desired link is to be found, there must be objects of aesthetic judgment that give rise to "intellectual interest" arising from their excellence of "form alone." Aesthetic judgment of this sort, were it possible, would not only supply the sought for systematic transition between sensual enjoyment and moral feeling; it would also reestablish disinterested *pleasure* (along with the other three moments of beauty) as taste's proper witness,[34] and thereby reaffirm the autonomy of taste under conditions that otherwise tend to undermine it.

3 Artistic Beauty

Kant's treatment of artistic beauty has proved especially troubling to critics,[35] both for its apparent failure to conform to the strict "formalism" of his earlier account and, relatedly, for fine art's evident reliance, contrary to his earlier strictures with regard to "pure judgments of taste," on some concept (or concepts) of what something is "to be." Moreover, his deflationary discussion of "adherent" beauty (under which "fine art" is frequently subsumed) seems inadequate to explain the artistic "exemplarity" to which the sections on "fine art [*schöne Kunst*]"[36] are specifically devoted. I will argue that Kant's treatment of artistic beauty – once due allowance is made for the peculiar nature of its norm – is both more compelling on its face and more consistent with the argument that precedes it than is sometimes thought.

Section #41 had shown why the "empirical interest" in beauty that is connected with the natural inclination to society offers only an "ambiguous"

---

[33] See especially Guyer (1979), though he later adopts a more expansive position (Guyer, 1997).
[34] Compare Halper (2020).   [35] See, for example, Guyer (1979); but compare Guyer (1997).
[36] Also translatable as "beautiful art."

transition between sensual pleasure and moral feeling (*CJ* 5:297–98).[37] Nor does the "intellectual interest" in the beautiful described in #42 suffice for such a purpose. For that intellectual interest not only lacks any clear relation to our natural inclination to society; it also presupposes the very moral cultivation that our empirical interest in the beautiful manifestly puts at risk. If the sought transition between the sensual and the moral is to be found, it would seem that the refinement of taste (including a taste for fine art) to which civilization inevitably gives rise must yield an interest that is "related to society" (*CJ* 5:299) yet irreducible to the desire for sensual pleasure.

What is still missing, then, is a standard of beauty and accompanying a priori principle of taste that apply to works of art directly (as in "fine/beautiful art") rather than merely "conditionally," as with "adherent beauties" as earlier described.[38] Such a standard, were it possible, would help restore disinterested pleasure, as distinguished from "mere social joys" (*CJ* 5:300), to its rightful place as the first criterion of beauty. A taste for fine art might thereby not only prove more resistant to being "melted down" (*CJ* 5:298) but also yield an interest that could vindicate the process of civilization in the face of Rousseau's powerful critique.

And yet any such prospect faces an immediate difficulty. Judgments of natural beauty apply to objects whose "form" was given, as it were, by nature and hence whose possibility did not presuppose a determinate concept of what the thing "is to be." Works of art, by contrast, are possible only through the conscious actions of a free being, from whose concept of an end they derive their "form." How, then, can the formal "purposiveness without purpose" that defines judgments of beauty generally be reconciled with the recognition of an object as a work of *art*, and hence as deriving its form through a freely chosen end?

Such a norm of taste would have to accommodate the "purposiveness" peculiar to a work of art. Nor is this all: Its universality would also have to apply more narrowly than with free beauties of nature; for the appreciation of artful beauty depends for its "perfection," as Kant here indicates, on acquaintance with specific languages and customs as well as knowledge and skill that presumes an advanced level of civilization (*CJ* 5:305, 312). Such a norm would thus of necessity be more aspirational than descriptive; and its accompanying idea of "common sense" would similarly be best conceived as a goal, achievable, perhaps, historically, rather than (as with judgments of free beauties of nature) as "original and natural."

---

[37] Compare Guyer (1993:257–58).

[38] For a more detained consideration of the relation between free beauties of nature and the beauty of fine art see Reuger (2008). For Reuger, exemplary works are also "free beauties," whereas for Guyer (1997), among others, they are "adherent." My own view as to Kant's meaning is that they are neither "free" in a sense covered by the deduction at #38 nor "adherent" in the sense of being conditional on the perfection of their object. (There can be a beautiful representation of a dying horse or a ruined church.)

Finally, it would apply not only to the judging of individual works of fine art but also to our acquisition of a taste fully adequate to this task.

Sections #43–50 sketch the conditions of the possibility of such a regulative norm, beginning with the requirements of art in general (#43) and culminating in discussion of the relation between genius and taste – each necessary, albeit in different ways, to both the recognition and the production of artful beauty (i.e., exemplary works of fine art). And they raise a problem that any such norm must also address: namely, a certain tendency of our pleasure in artful beauty to flag over time (*CJ* 5:326; cf. 5:322).

In #43 and #44 Kant provides a taxonomic map that pinpoints the distinctiveness of representations to which such a norm of judgment might apply: first, they must be products of *freedom*, deriving their *form* from *human skill*, rather than from nature directly (*CJ* 5:303). Second, they must be works of *art*, understood as a *practical* skill, rather than of *science* (where to know is already to be able to make) (*CJ* 5:303). Third, application of the skill must be "liberal" or "free," – that is, it must be regarded as if it could turn out purposefully or succeed only as "play," and as "an occupation agreeable in itself" rather than as "remunerative" or desirable only for the sake of something else, although something "compulsory" is required as well lest the "spirit" of the work evaporate into nothing (*CJ* 5:304). Fourth, the liberal art in question must also be "aesthetic"; that is, it must have as its immediate aim, not the production of an object to which the artist's concept is adequate (which would render the art "mechanical"), but "the feeling of pleasure." But fifth, the pleasure cannot be merely that of the agreeable, whose standard would be "mere sensation." Such pleasure might give rise to "momentary entertainment," including social pleasures that help "time pass unnoticed." But it would not leave behind "matter" [*Stoff*] for later thought and speech [*Nachdenken und Nachreden*]. The disinterested aesthetic pleasure to which fine art in its perfection gives rise, by way of contrast, will prove, on critical analysis, to "[cultivate] the forces of the mind" (*CJ* 5:306) – albeit without aiming at it directly (cf. *CJ* 5:329).

How, then, is an a priori principle suitable for the judgment of beautiful or fine art possible?[39] Given what has already been shown, fine art, no less than natural beauty, must "*please in the mere judging*," that is, "neither in sensation nor through a concept" (*CJ* 5:306). Hence, although it "certainly

---

[39] Compare Rogerson (2008:41–43). My own position is that the constitutive principle of taste that is adequate for judging natural beauty is a necessary but not sufficient condition for the judging of exemplary works of art. While Kant will later say that even beauties of nature "can [*kann*] . . . be regarded as the expression of aesthetic ideas" (*CJ* 5:320) he does not say that they *must* be so regarded in order to be judged beautiful. On the latter point, compare Allison (2001:286) and Zuckert (2007:202).

is intentional," it must not "seem" to be, but must be recognized as art without signs showing through that rules have fettered the mental forces of the artist (*CJ* 5:307). Such a work must appear other than it is (or purposive without purpose and yet somehow intentional) without actually deceiving us (unlike the birdsong that ceases to please once its artificial source is recognized [*CJ* 5:243]).

3.1 Genius, Taste, and Spirit

This paradoxical demand is met by "genius," provisionally defined at #46 as the "inborn productive faculty," or "predisposition of the mind (*ingenium*) *through which* nature gives the rule to art" (*CJ* 5:307). Every art "presupposes rules that first lay the ground by means of which a product that is to be called artful is first represented as possible." Hence, fine art too must have its rules, albeit ones that do not arise from a determinate concept (as with the carpenter's concept of a chair) but that lie in "the nature of the subject" of an artist who is endowed with genius (*CJ* 5:344).

Genius has four elements: first, the artist's ideas must come to him "originally," or directly from nature. Second, his work must be "exemplary" (*CJ* 5:308), serving others as a standard for judging that the artist can communicate but not state. But third, the artist cannot pass along his method to others by means of determinate rules (as a scientist like Newton can), in such a way as to make continual progress possible (*CJ* 5:309). Hence, and fourth, his work can only serve as a model for "succession" by those naturally endowed with a "similar proportion of mental forces," and for "imitation" (but not copying) by others including lesser artists who form "schools."

The artist as genius was a well-worn figure of eighteenth-century aesthetics, especially associated in Germany with Herder.[40] Kant here appropriates that discourse to his own ends, charting a course between the enthusiastic excesses (as Kant saw them) of the Herder "genius cult" and the rule-dominated scholasticism of the conventional academy.[41] "Genius" reconciles two apparently opposing demands: namely, that "every art presupposes rules" and that judgment of an object as "beautiful" should not be derived "from any rule that has a determinate concept as its ground" (*CJ* 5:307).

In justifying the latter claim, Kant draws on the then fashionable opinion[42] that genius and "the *spirit of imitation*" are "entirely opposed." Artists who are

---

[40] For a helpful summary, see Burdick (2010). Kant may also be responding to Alexander Gerard's *Essay on Genius*, which appeared in German in 1776.

[41] For an instructive history of the term, see McMahon (2013). See also Tonelli's (1966) classic study of Kant's own early usage.

[42] Labio (2004) gives a useful historical account.

naturally endowed with genius do not "imitate" nature (as Aristotle held) but instead "succeed" (*nachfolgen*) others of like talent who precede them (*CJ* 5:308).[43] Two factors here are noteworthy: first, the artist's ignorance of how, in the absence of a determinate concept, thought and fancy "come together" in his mind, or by what process the "idea" in which they are united comes to him. A second factor is art's non-progressive character; for whereas with science, effort and imitation can often substitute for sudden discovery, with fine art nothing can replace genius as a source of ideas whose rules cannot be communicated directly (since the artist himself is not consciously aware of them) but that can be "abstracted" from the deed by others – including fledgling artists in whom the proportion of mental forces is similarly favorable (*CJ* 5:309).

Being deemed the product of genius, then, is a condition of the possibility of a thing being judged aesthetically as both a work of art and also beautiful (*CJ* 5:307), given Kant's earlier analysis of judgments of taste. And like that earlier analysis, Kant's discussion here has a double aim: For by clarifying the necessary meaning of fine art he also steers readers away from several common errors of judgment that conceptual confusion tends to encourage, for example, that native talent is all that matters.

For genius alone is not enough. If an object is to be regarded as a product of beautiful *art*, it must also (be understood to) be grounded in a concept (as a chair is grounded in the concept of its maker), albeit a concept that does not give rise to determinate rules that would allow the artist to repeat his activity at will or communicate his method of invention to others. These rules, moreover, are of two kinds. First, the artist must acquire the taste to judge his own work. He must therefore be academically trained or otherwise acquaint himself with exemplary models whose rules cannot be stated but only "abstracted from the deed" for purposes of either "succession" or "imitation." For only by acquiring such a taste can the artist "work up" the "matter"[44] furnished by genius into an enduring "*form*" that "stand[s] up to [*bestehen*] the power of judgment" (*CJ* 5:310).

---

[43] According to Grimm and Grimm (1854), the basic meaning of "*nachfolgen*" is "to follow after" or "in sequence" as in the "imitation" of Christ (*Matthew* 16:24) which Luther's Bible renders using this term. For an informed discussion of links between Kant's understanding of succession and the contemporary German appreciation of Milton, see Burdick (2010). (Burdick's erroneous rendering [p.1] of "*Nachahmung*" as "succession" is symptomatic of a more general undervaluing of taste's positive contribution to works of genius; cf. *CJ* 5:309.) On Kant's earlier understanding of the demands of genius, see also Dyck (2004).

[44] As Guyer (1997:297) observes, both the judgment and production of fine art are not without matter or content. I would add that what is "essential" is still the formal relation of harmony between imagination, understanding, and – in the case of exemplary products of art – reason as well.

Second, insofar as it is *artful* beauty it must be grounded in a *concept or intention*, and hence must "pay regard" to "what an object is to be," that is, to its "perfection." But what the artist intends to make is a beautiful "representation" of something. Or as Kant states, whereas a beauty of nature "is a *beautiful thing*," a beauty of art "is a *beautiful representation* of a thing" (*CJ* 5:311).[45] Thus fine art shows its excellence precisely by beautifully representing that which in real life would be ugly, for example, death and war (*CJ* 5:312). This evidence for the subjectively mediated character of artful beauty, which lies not in the thing represented but the representation itself, also distinguishes fine art from adherent beauties as earlier described (*CJ* 5:229), whose beauty was dependent on the perfection of its object either for purposes of use (as with beautiful churches) or for purposes internal to them (as with beautiful horses).[46] Kant makes an exception, however, to his general rule as to how artful beauty proves its specific excellence that he will later apply to fine art itself (cf. *CJ* 5:326): No artist can represent beautifully what arouses "disgust" (*Ekel*). For in this case, the object is represented as "imposing an enjoyment" that we at the same time "forcibly resist" thanks to a sensation arising from "sheer imagination," and we can no longer distinguish between the representation and the sensation that is represented (*CJ* 5:312).

Now the intention of the artist presumably includes communication of that concept to others. And what is essential in fine art is the form (*CJ* 5:326). Hence the "beautiful representation of an object,"[47] as Kant summarizes, is "properly only the form of the presentation of a concept by which the latter is universally communicated" (*CJ* 5:312). To give this form to a work of fine art requires, however, merely taste "to which the artist . . . holds up his work, and after many, often arduous, attempts finds the form that satisfies him . . . [and thus] make[s] the work adequate to the thought . . . without damaging the free play of the forces of the mind" (*CJ* 5:312).

This free play, or rather "impetus" (*Schwung*), is the result of another factor Kant has yet to mention: namely, "spirit" (*Geist*) in an "aesthetic sense," or "the animating principle of the mind" (*CJ* 5:313). This requirement points to a difference between the mental animation that is typical of judgments of natural beauty and that involved in judgments of fine art. Thus a work can be in

---

[45] See also Guyer (1997:356). Aiming to please, however, as Guyer also notes, does not exhaust the meaning of the artist's "concept" or "intention," which includes presentation, through aesthetic "expression" and "expansion," of either an idea of reason or some other appropriate concept (such as love). Kant does not say that judgments of fine art do not involve concepts but merely that they cannot depend on rules that have a concept as their "determining ground" (*CJ* 5:307).

[46] See also the helpful discussion in Allison (2001:295–98).

[47] See also Allison (2001:275–78) and Zuckert (2007:184–86).

conformity to taste (in the sense necessary to feel the "free harmony" of imagination and understanding) and still lack "spirit." To be sure, no one expects spirit from useful items (such as table settings and sermons) in which "beautiful form merely" is not valued for itself but serves only as a vehicle of communication. But in a work intended as fine art – even one in which one finds "nothing to reproach" as touches upon taste – lack of spirit is a fatal defect (*CJ* 5:313).

Spirit imparts not just a "movement" (*Bewegung*) that is "self-maintaining and self-strengthening" (*CJ* 5:222) (as with the reciprocal animation of imagination and understanding associated with judgments of natural beauty) but an "impetus" (*Schwung*)[48] that *also* "strengthens [the forces of the mind] to that effect" (*CJ* 5:313). And it is accordingly "purposive" not only for cognition as such (as with judgments of natural beauty) but also for "cultivating the forces of the mind for sociable communication" (*CJ* 5:306).[49]

The "matter" through whose presentation spirit imparts such impetus Kant calls "aesthetic ideas."[50] An aesthetic idea is a "representation of the imagination which occasions much thought without any determinate thought or concept being adequate to it." As such it is the "counterpart" to a rational idea, that is, a concept to which no intuition corresponds. Kant had in earlier *Critiques* used "idea" only in reference to concepts of reason. Extension of that term to representations of the imagination is appropriate, he claims here, mainly because "no concept can be fully adequate to them as inner intuitions" but also because "they at least strive to go beyond the bounds of experience and thus to come near the presentation of concepts of reason (rational ideas)." Our productive imagination is "very mighty in the creation [*Schaffung*], as it were, of another nature out of the matter that the real one gives us": "We entertain ourselves with them when experience becomes too every-day; to be sure we so . . . form [*bilden*] these according to analogous laws, but also in according to principles that lie higher up in reason (and that are as natural as those by which understanding comprehends empirical nature)" (*CJ* 5:314). We amuse ourselves, in other words, with imagined possibilities that combine in an indeterminate way both the limits of empirical nature and the requirements of reason; and we thereby

---

[48] Compare *P* 4:317. Kant had earlier used both "Geist" and "Schwung" with respect to the sublime (e.g., at *CJ* 5:262, 272, 274).

[49] See also Fugate (2009:617–18) on the difference between mere liveliness and genius as a ground or "principle" of life.

[50] For both Rogerson (2008) and Chignell (2007), Kant's doctrine of aesthetic ideas is necessary to resolve the respective problems of free harmony and particularity. On my reading, related issues of universality and necessity are still outstanding only in the case of exemplary works of art (and beauties of nature insofar as they arouse aesthetic ideas).

"feel our freedom" from the "law of association" on which "imagination depends in its empirical use" (*CJ* 5:314).

This striving on the part of the imagination, which in most of us amounts to little more than capricious entertainment (cf. *CJ* 5:335), is in an artist both more artful and more "dignified" and "earnest" (*CJ* 5:335). The poet, for example (in whose art this power of the imagination reveals its "full measure"), "dares to sensualize rational ideas" such as "eternity" and "invisible beings," which may be but are not necessarily moral.[51] And he also ventures "to make sensible beyond the limits of experience" concepts that are exemplified experientially (e.g., envy and love) with a "completeness" that "emulates reason's foreplay [*Vernunft= Vorspiele*] in attaining to a maximum" (*CJ* 5:314).[52] In that case too, imagination's aesthetic idea calls to mind a rational idea (in, so to speak, sensible form).

But the presentation of aesthetic ideas is in itself merely a "talent" to which the artist must contribute means of "expression" (*Ausdruck*) by which his concept (i.e., what he means to present) can be communicated to others.[53] This he accomplishes by adding to the concept a representation that "belongs to its presentation" but that by itself also "induces so much thinking that it can never be contained in a determinate concept" (*CJ* 5:315). If the artist wishes to present the "majesty of creation," for example, he may represent the claws and arrows of Jupiter, which elicit an unbounded series of related thoughts that bear on creation by affinity or as possible consequences, thereby "enlarging" the concept itself to include more than understanding can determinately comprehend. In so doing, imagination becomes "creative" (*schöpferisch*) in a sense Kant no longer qualifies (as at *CJ* 5:314); and it thereby "brings into movement [*Bewegung*] the faculty of intellectual ideas (reason)" (*CJ* 5:315).

Kant calls such representations "aesthetic attributes," that is, attributes of an object "to whose concept, as an idea of reason, no presentation can be adequate" (*CJ* 5:315). Such attributes do not belong to the object directly (as do logical attributes) but instead "cause imagination to spread over a vast number [*Menge*] of affined representations that cannot be grasped in a concept determined by speech" (*CJ* 5:315). And this yields, in turn, an aesthetic idea in the mind of the

---

[51] See also Matherne (2013) and Chignell (2007). Chignell reads Kant's treatment of aesthetic ideas and aesthetic symbolization of the moral as also applying to judgment of free beauties. For Geiger (2021), on the other hand, all fine art is a presentation of "the idea of humanity in our person."

[52] Both *"nacheifern"* and *"Vorspiele"* are unusual if not unique terms in Kant's published writings. *"Eifern"* means "to earnestly strive." *"Vorspiele"* can also be translated as "prologue" or "prelude" – that is, as initiating a process of completion that can never be attained.

[53] For a fuller discussion, see Matherne (2013); see also Zuckert (2007:184).

receptive audience, whose forces of imagination and understanding assume a similar mutually sustaining and strengthening impetus.[54] Such an aesthetic idea "serves" the rational idea, albeit indirectly and only to "animate the mind"; for if one were made aware of this intention (e.g., in a poem whose "moral" is too intrusive) one would no longer find the presentation beautiful (i.e., purposive without purpose).

Genius comprehensively considered is thus the "fortunate relation" – incommunicable by determinate rules – between "finding aesthetic ideas" for a given concept and "coming upon the *expression* of these by which the subjective disposition of the mind [*Gemüthsstimmung*] thus effected can be communicated to others" (*CJ* 5:317).[55]

3.2 The King's Speech

Given these high claims, one is struck by Kant's sparing reference in the Critique of Taste to what he regards as artists worthy of fulfilling them. Indeed, his only extended examples of "aesthetic attributes" are themselves singularly unimpressive. One is drawn from an "academic" verse sufficiently commonplace to be cited in a popular dictionary.[56] The other is taken from a poem by "the great king" (Frederick the Great) on "the vain terrors of death and fears of another life" in "imitation . . . of Lucretius."[57] Kant not only refrains from calling either piece "exemplary"; he also makes no mention here of the "aesthetic ideas" whose peculiar relation to aesthetic attributes mark, as we have seen, the true work of genius.

Kant may avoid reference (other than in passing at *CJ* 5:309) to exemplary artists like Milton, whom he elsewhere praises (*Anth* 7:231), lest he inhibit the aesthetic autonomy of his readers (cf. *CJ* 5:286). But he may also mean to encourage us thereby to exercise our own powers of discernment (e.g., in distinguishing works that have spirit from those that are at best merely tasteful[58]) in ways that bear on political life more directly.

---

[54] See Rogerson (2008:21).   [55] Compare Guyer (1997:360).

[56] The lines are from *Akademischen Gedichten* [Academic Poems] by Phillip Lorenz Withot (1725–89).

[57] Critics have generally refrained from commenting on Kant's use of Frederick's verse other than to express mild puzzlement. But compare Allison (2001:287).

[58] On my reading, such merely tasteful work satisfies the ("constitutive") requirement of free harmony between imagination and understanding, but no more. In the case of an exemplary work, by way of contrast, imagination not only conforms to the laws of understanding (if only by analogy [*CJ* 5:314, 327]) but also "serves" (*CJ* 5:329) understanding, by "nourishing" it (*CJ* 5:321), for example. Without this qualification, it is difficult to see how a work that aimed to be fine art could be "irreproachable" with regard to "taste" and yet, as Kant insists (at *CJ* 5:313), fall short of the demands of fine art proper.

Frederick's poem is part of a longer work of epistolary verse that Kant here reproduces, albeit with significant changes.[59] These include both translation of the French original into German prose and a moralizing alteration of the final line:

> Let us depart from life without complaining and without anything to regret in leaving behind the world afterwards piled high with boons [*Wohlthaten*]. Thus the sun, after completing its daily course, still spreads a gentle light across the heavens and the last rays that it sends into the air are its last sighs [*Seufzer*] for the wellbeing [*Wohl*] of the world. (*CJ* 5:316)

The author, as Kant goes on to say, thereby "animates *his* rational idea of a cosmopolitan disposition even at the end of life" through an attribute that imagination assigns to this representation (*CJ* 5:316; emphasis added). Frederick's original lines had read: "sont les derniers soupirs qu'il donne a l'univers" [are the last sighs that he gives to the universe]. In changing the original "universe" to the "wellbeing of the world" Kant gives the poem a less epicurean ending.[60] And Kant's use of a possessive pronoun (as in "his idea"), rather than the definite article that one might expect, draws additional attention to the possible divergence of their respective ideas of a "cosmopolitan disposition."

Frederick had dedicated his verse to James Francis Edward Keith, for whose heroic death at the Battle of Potsdam Frederick was partly to blame. That fact both colors the poem's general praise of courageous indifference toward death and qualifies the "boons" that Frederick could honestly regard himself as leaving behind, inasmuch as they include the unnecessary perishing of someone who was both an able field marshal and a personal friend.

Kant's *Anthropology* provides further reason to suspect an element of irony in his choice of Frederick's verse as his sole extended treatment of aesthetic attributes in situ, as it were (*Anth* 7:33 n.). He there wonders: "Why is "a mediocre poem [. . .] intolerable but a mediocre speech [*Rede*] still quite bearable? The cause seems to lie in the fact that the solemnity of tone in the poetic product arouses great expectation, and when these are not satisfied its value usually sinks even lower than the prosaic version might well deserve" (*Anth* 7:248–49).And yet, as Kant proceeds to add, the final verses of such poems may partially redeem the "staleness" [*Schale*] of the whole when they are retained as "aphorisms" that impart a "pleasant aftertaste" (*Anth* 7:250). Might Kant have deliberately altered Frederick's poem – both rendering it in

---

[59] Kant alters the Withof piece by replacing "goodness" with "virtue."

[60] Kant distinguishes elsewhere between boons that are regarded as burdens and those of a moral sort that warrant genuine gratitude (*MM* 6:456).

prose (even though modern poetry, as Kant elsewhere insists, should rhyme [*Anth* 7:248]) and adding a conclusion more consistent with a truly cosmopolitan attitude – with such an end in view?

With the sole exception of the *Anthropology*'s final note (*Anth* 7:333 n.), Kant was always circumspect in criticizing Frederick directly; and in any case his rapidly souring relations with the current monarch might have supplied another motive for drawing attention to "the great king," in favorable contrast with the new one. But the most telling evidence of Kant's irony in taking his only extended "example" (*Beifall*) of an aesthetic attribute from a model that he never calls "exemplary" (*exemplarisch*) may lie in his subsequent presentation of rhetoric as the aesthetically and morally ambiguous counterpart of poetry. For rhetoric (*Beredsamkeit*) *too*, according to Kant, "takes the spirit that animates [its] work" solely "from the aesthetic attributes of the objects that go alongside the logical ones" (*CJ* 5:315). And yet the "art of persuasion" (as we shall shortly see) counts as a "fine art" in a peculiar sense – one that touches, indeed, on the larger civilizational problem that Kant has been addressing all along.

Before turning to that larger issue, a review of the argument thus far with respect to fine art generally may prove helpful. Judgments of exemplary artistic beauty are not only characterized by *disinterestedness* (Moment One) (though they may allow "great interest" to be taken in them);[61] they are also determined by a communicable *Stimmung* of the mind that exhibits *purposiveness without purpose* (Moment Three). Although an exemplary work of art is necessarily conceived, as with any product of freedom, as *intentionally* purposive, it *also* permits itself to be regarded as purposive "unintentional[ly]," or without depending on a determinate rule or concept, for the animation of the cognitive faculties as a whole. Its specific "perfection" is therefore neither one of external utility (as with churches) nor supersensible artfulness (as with horses). In short, imagination is genuinely "creative," and hence freer than either in judgments of natural beauty,[62] in which imagination need not fabricate "another nature," or in judgments of adherent beauty, which are conditional on the perfection of the object for some purpose other than pleasing aesthetically. Nor does judgment of fine art require a force of imagination bordering on genius, as in judging ideal beauty (cf. *CJ* 5:236).

---

[61] Although judgments of taste of themselves "do not give rise to any interest" (*CJ* 5:205 n.), they may "allow" for "great interest" being taken in them (*CJ* 5:236) – interest, however, that "cannot be inferred," as Kant puts it, from "the mere reflective power of judgment" (*CJ* 5:296), that is (on my reading), from the constitutive principle of taste alone.

[62] Compare Ostaric (2017).

At the same time, in both the production and judging of exemplary artistic beauty the productive imagination gives understanding more than it can grasp, thereby bringing into motion reason itself, whose ideas it "serves" albeit without conscious intention.[63] Accordingly, works of genius – despite their lack of "purity" as earlier defined – give expression to a "feeling of [mental] unity" more comprehensive and hence formally more perfect than are natural beauties, as Kant had indeed earlier admitted (*CJ* 5:299–300).[64] Might that form give rise, "if only indirectly," to an "interest" capable of supplying the sought for "transition" from the sensually agreeable to the good (*CJ* 5:295–96)? If so, it might also help account for the stronger version of taste's claim – that is, as a "demand" bordering on "duty" (*CJ* 5:296–97). And it might accordingly fill in the missing "moments" (under the respective headings of Quantity and Modality) that are necessary if an a priori principle of taste with respect to works of fine art is to be adequately justified.

Taste with respect to fine art "brings clarity and order to the fullness of thought and thus makes ideas tenable [*haltbar*]" and hence an example for succession that is "suitable for an ever-progressing culture" (*CJ* 5:319). And yet such discipline, as we later learn, must itself be subjected to "sharp critique [*scharfe Kritik*]" lest it also smother the "freedom of imagination in its lawfulness" without which neither fine art nor even proper taste for judging it is possible (*CJ* 5:355).

Artful beauty thus has a downside missing from its natural counterpart, whose disinterested pleasures do not ebb so long as one is introduced to them when young. At the same time pleasure in fine art is also "culture." It thus contributes to our "urbanity," making the spirit "receptive to many kinds of pleasure and entertainment" that would otherwise remain unfamiliar (*CJ* 5:326). And yet if works of art arouse mainly pleasures of enjoyment – owing either to their own aesthetic deficiencies or those of their audience – "[they leave] the spirit dull" and the object "by and by disgusting" (*CJ* 5:326). Useful objects can and sometimes should be tasteful (e.g., table settings and sermons). But if works that aim to be fine art are not also *exemplary* (or their exemplarity is not appreciated) – if they "leave nothing behind in the idea" and instead "serve only for

---

[63] Compare, in this regard, the feeling of the sublime, in which imagination "presents" a rational idea by failing to meet the demands of understanding, rather than (as here) by prompting a failure of comprehension on the latter's part.

[64] Although such judgments involve a concept of what something is to be and hence are not "pure" in the sense of being "independent of a concept of the object" (*CJ* 5:288: cf. *CJ* 5:226, 279, 288, 289–90, 296, 301), judgments of fine art involve "as pure a liking" (*CJ* 5:353) and are hence "pure" in the sense of not depending on an interest. On this point, compare Tuna (2018) and Guyer (2005:161–62).

diversion" – they soon cease to please aesthetically (*CJ* 5:326). It is no wonder, then, that the refinement of taste so often leads to taste being melted down with sensual pleasures, and (hence) to the social corruption (cf. *CJ* 5:328) of which Rousseau warned.

What is needed, then, is a critically informed a priori principle that would better guide us in acquiring and sustaining a taste for artistic beauty. And yet, for reasons we have seen, the universality and necessity of such judgments are problematic in a way that the universality and necessity of judgments of free natural beauty are not.[65]

Nor, as Kant makes clear, are the rules of thought that apply to "common sense" in the sense of *common understanding* a sufficient guide; for it is not *thinking*, with its concomitant commitment to objective proof, but *feeling*, that is here at issue.[66] Whether there is indeed a principle of taste (i.e., an "idea of common sense") for artful beauty that can lay justified claim to the necessary assent of everyone still remains an open question, one that only the "science of criticism" (*CJ* 5:286) here on offer can resolve.

4 Rhetoric and the Antinomy of Taste

4.1 Rhetoric and Poetry

Kant initially defines rhetoric [*Beredsamkeit*] as the "art of conducting a business of the understanding as a free play of the imagination," whereas poetry "carr[ies] out a free play of imagination as a business of the understanding." Rhetoric so understood is inherently deceptive.[67] It promises more than it delivers, while poetry, by contrast, gives "nourishment" to the understanding and "life" to its concepts under the guise of "play" (*CJ* 5:321).

Commentators have typically taken Kant's negative evaluation of rhetoric at face value.[68] Several provocative recent readings (including Stroud [2014], Ercolini [2016], and Leeten [2019]), however, have challenged the conventional view and suggested a more nuanced position on Kant's part. These readings draw attention to his own distinction between "rhetoric" (*Beredsamkeit, ars oratoria*) as "the art of persuading" (*Kunst zu überrreden*) and what he calls "mere skill in speaking (eloquence and style)" (*blosse Wohlredenheit* [*Eloquenz und Stil*]) (*CJ* 5:327). The picture that emerges suggests not only a more positive view of "excellence in speech" but also Kant's extended engagement with both

---

[65] See also Rogerson (2008:208–9); compare Dyck (2004).

[66] Compare Matherne (2019), who models aesthetic education mainly on the rules of thinking that Kant associates with the *sensus communis logicus*.

[67] See also (*Refl-A* 15:436 [#991]). For a helpful review of the recent literature, see Pasquiere (2020).

[68] For example, Dostal (1980), Garsten (2006), Abbott (2007).

Cicero and Quintilian,[69] along with contemporaries such as Johann Christoph Gottsched,[70] whose *Comprehensive Art of Speech* (*Ausführliche Redekunst*) had until recently figured prominently in the curriculum of German universities, Kant's included.[71]

There is, of course, a long tradition, beginning with Plato, of philosophic objections to rhetoric on both theoretical and practical grounds. At the same time, its qualified reprisal by Aristotle, Cicero, and others (and, indeed, by Plato himself) is itself an important theme in the history of philosophy both ancient and modern. Hobbes' own highly rhetorical attack on rhetoric set the tone for later Enlightenment authors, whose appeal to the peace loving peace-loving "passions" of fear, sympathy, and the desire for material comfort made a new sort of rhetoric an essential tool of politics, even as such authors denounced both the classical rhetorical tradition for its undue emphasis upon the martial virtues and the spiritually inflated language of the Church. Gottshed, in general keeping with the Ciceronian tradition, had distinguished between a rationally (and morally) guided "eloquentia," and "rhetorica," understood as a body of oral and literary techniques that could, at times, be misused. In distinguishing between what he understood as negative and positive kinds of rhetoric, Kant was engaging, then, with a series of sometimes opposing arguments that would generally have been familiar to his audience, who would have been in a position to recognize the peculiarity of his claims.

Kant's position on the specific superiority of poetry (and the accompanying ambiguity of rhetoric) emerges most clearly in his comparison of the "aesthetic value" of the various fine arts. Among these, poetry occupies first place.

> The art of poetry (which owes its origin almost entirely to genius and will be guided least by prescript or example) maintains the highest rank. It expands [*erweitert*] the mind by setting the imagination free and working up [*darbei-ten*], within the limits of a given concept and among the unbounded manifold of forms possibly agreeing with it, the one whose exhibition is connected with a fullness of thoughts [*Gedankenfülle*] to which no linguistic expression [*Sprachausdruck*] is fully adequate, and thus elevates itself [*sich . . . erhebt*] to ideas. It *strengthens the mind*, in letting it feel its capacity – one that is free,

---

[69] Both Garsten and Stroud treat Garve, both as *Popularphilosoph* and in his capacity as a conduit of Ciceronian rhetoric, as Kant's main adversary here. In treating Garve as Kant's sole significant interlocutor Stroud neglects Rousseau, to whose own opposition, in the former's favor, of persuasion to conviction Kant is also implicitly responding.

[70] See Leteen (2019).

[71] As Leteen observes, Gottsched's *Comprehensive Doctrine* provided the theoretical foundation for his two textbooks on rhetoric: *Preliminary Studies of Eloquence* (*Vorübungen der Beredsamkeit*, 1754), which served as a grammar school handbook, and *Academic Art of Speech* (*Akademische Redekunst*, 1759), which was the standard German university textbook on a subject required at Kant's university until 1788.

self-active, and independent of natural determination – to consider and judge nature as appearance in accordance with points of view [*Ansichten*] that nature by itself does not work up in experience for either sensibility or understanding, and thus to use [nature] for the sake of and as it were for a schema of the supersensible. (*CJ* 5:326; emphasis added)

In this remarkable passage, Kant highlights the characteristics that allow a taste for artful beauty to contribute to "an ever-progressing culture" (*CJ* 5:319) in a way that an untutored taste for free beauties of nature cannot similarly accomplish. Those characteristics include the exhibition, among the "unbounded manifold of forms" for which the productive imagination (rather than mere nature) is responsible, of one "that is connected with a fullness of thoughts" that not only enlivens the forces of the mind but "strengthens" it (*CJ* 5:326).[72] By contrast, rhetoric "insofar as it is understood as the art of persuading [*Übrredung*]," not only fails to give rise to a feeling of the mind's capacity for self-active independence; it also, under the guise of what Kant calls "beautiful semblance [*Schein*],"[73] *deprives* minds of their freedom in the very act of seeming to do otherwise. Rhetoric so understood is thus a "dialectic" that "cannot be recommended for either the courtroom or the pulpit"; for it "borrows enough from the art of poetry as is necessary to win over minds to the advantage of the speaker before they can judge and takes away their freedom" (*CJ* 5:327).

Kant's treatment in the *Jaosoho Looturos* of the difference between persuasion and conviction sheds further light on how rhetoric takes away the listener's freedom in the guise of doing otherwise. Conviction (*Überzeugung*) is a "holding to be true" (*Fürwahrhalten*) on grounds that one knows to be "certain," be it objectively or subjectively (i.e., in a "practical" way). Persuasion (*Überredung*), on the other hand, is a holding to be true whose grounds remain opaque (*JL* 9:72–73).[74] In order to pass successfully from persuasion to conviction, one would have to "investigate" those grounds (*JL* 9:73). And yet, the "reflect[ion]," and related "suspension" of one's judgment that such investigation would require, are both "difficult" and rare. This is so both because "inclination" rushes us to premature judgment, and because

---

[72] Consider Kant's implicit contrast between the role of the productive imagination in pure judgments of natural beauty and in poetic activity, in which imagination is no longer bound, as in the former case, to the "determinate form" of an "object [of nature]" (*CJ* 5:240–41).

[73] On the meaning of "semblance" (*Schein*) as distinguished from "appearance" (*Erscheinung*), see *MFNS* 4:555.

[74] Stroud's otherwise careful and informative study does not take sufficiently into account Kant's objection to "persuasion" *as such* (i.e., "however well intended or good in [its] effect"), inasmuch as it tends to undermine the listener's capacity for "reflection" (*CJ* 5:328, 462–63); cf. Stroud (2014:7, 45, 141; 2015:191).

"understanding" *itself* is so "*desirous [begierig] of expanding itself* [*sich zu erweitern*; emphasis added] . . . with new subjects of awareness [Kenntnissen]" [*JL* 9:74]). As a result, prejudices, whose first and most comprehensive cause is "imitation," do not serve as "true provisional judgments," as they should (*JL* 9:75), but are mistaken for "determining judgments" (*JL* 9:76). For although reason is an "active" principle, many people, out of intellectual "lassitude [*Trägheit*]," prefer to follow others rather than "strain the forces of their own understanding." And yet, Kant observes, if all people were content to be "copies," progress would be impossible. It is therefore, as he here concludes, "of the highest necessity and importance" that youths not be held to mere imitation, as customarily happens (*JL* 9:76).

Read in this light, cultivation of a taste for artful beauty (especially for poetry) assumes heightened significance. For such a taste not only counters the mind's inclination toward passivity; it also makes purposive an *active* drive toward self-expansion (*JL* 9:74) that otherwise tends to overreach itself. Rhetoric (*Beredsamkeit*), in contrast, not only indulges the mind's inclination toward passivity but does so by exploiting the very pleasure that tends by its own nature to resist it. If persuasion is "mere semblance [*Schein*]," in which "the ground of judgment, which lies entirely in the subject, is taken to be objective" [*CPR* A 820=B 848], persuasion as an *art beautifies* (*beschönigt*) that semblance (*CJ* 5:327).

To be sure, beautiful semblance is sometimes beneficial, as is the case with sexual modesty, where the accompanying masking of sexual desire prevents each sex from being reduced to a mere tool for the enjoyment of the other (*Anth* 7:152).[75] Still, once the proper principles have been discovered and internalized, semblance, as Kant puts it in the *Critique of Pure Reason*, must be "forcefully combatted" as a "weed among which good dispositions cannot grow" (*CPR* A 748=B 776).

The perniciousness of the art of rhetoric is insidious: Whereas poetry openly declares that it is merely an entertaining ploy, rhetoric presents itself under the deceptive guise of seriousness (*CJ* 5:327); and it thereby "stifles" rather than "nourish[es]" the mind. Nor, as concerns matters of the "court" or "pulpit," can legitimate ends justify resort to the "machinery of persuasion," as Ciceronians (such as Gottsched) urge. This is so not only because it is unnecessary (well-spokenness – i.e., euphony [*Wohllauts*] in speech and propriety [*Wohlanständigkeit*] in expression – always here sufficing), but also because as rhetoric it "can never entirely eradicate the secret suspicion of artful subterfuge [*künstliche Überlistung*]" (*CJ* 5:327). Thus, while Kant associates the art of rhetoric with the employment of "aesthetic attributes," he makes no similar mention of "aesthetic ideas."

---

[75] Compare *Rem* 20:48.

This omission is not surprising given rhetoric's negative effect on cognitive activity, including above all, the activity of reason.

In sum: persuasive rhetoric (*Beredsamkeit*) strikes the power of judgment at its weakest point by blocking the crucial "reflective" stage by which the mind normally advances from provisional opinion to well-grounded conviction. And it is especially damaging in matters of "civil laws" and individual "rights," as well as the "instruction and determination of minds to correct knowledge and conscientious observation of one's duty," that is, where rational guidance of the faculty of judgment is of particular moral and civil importance (*CJ* 5:327). To underscore this, Kant adds an unusually personal note:

> I must admit that a beautiful poem has always given me pure enjoyment [*reines Vergnügen*], whereas the reading of the best speech [*Rede*] of a Roman popular speaker or a contemporary speaker in parliament or the pulpit has always been mixed with the disagreeable feeling of disapproval of a deceitful [*hinterlistigen*] art that understands how to move human beings, like machines, to a judgment in important things that in calm afterthought [*Nachdenken*] must lose all weight with them. Eloquence [*Beredheit*] and well-spokenness (together, rhetoric [*Rhetorik*]) belong to fine art; but the art of speech [*Rednerkunst*] (ars oratoria), as the art of making the weakness of human beings serve one's own aims (however well intended or good in their effect),[76] is worthy of no *respect* at all .... One who has under his control [*Gewalt*], along with clear insight into the facts, language in its richness and purity, and who along with a fruitful imagination capable of exhibiting his ideas, has a lively sharing of the heart [*Herzenantheil*] in the true good, is the *vir bonus dicendi peritus*, the speaker without art [*Redner ohne Kunst*] but with full expression [*Nachdruck*], as Cicero would have him, without himself having always remained faithful to this ideal. (*CJ* 5:327–28 n.)

Beginning with a statement of (merely) personal taste, Kant ends by suggesting that there may be a genuinely laudable way of speaking (*reden*) that improves upon both the theory and the practice of the ancients.

Kant here inverts the terminological distinction, common to the Aristotelian–Ciceronian tradition, between "rhetoric" (*ars rhetorica*) as a mere tool that can be used for good or ill and "oratory" (*ars oratorica*) that is both rationally guided and always laudable. By contrast, he identifies "oratory" (*Beredsamkeit*; *ars oratoria*) with a persuasive art, or "dialectic," that, however well-intentioned or benign in its effect, deserves "no *respect* at all." And he reserves "rhetoric" (*Rhetorik*) for a combination of fluency (*Beredheit*) and well-spokenness (*Wohlredenheit*) that

---

[76] Compare Gottsched, *Ausführliche Redekunst*, 51–53 and Gottsched, *Akademische Redekunst, zum Gebrauche der Vorlesungen auf hohen Schulen als ein bequemes Handbuch eingerichtet und mit den schönsten Zeugnissen der Alten erläutert* (Leipzig: Breitkopf, 1759), 28f., quoted in Leteen (2019:69).

he considers at home "[among] the fine art[s]" (*CJ* 5:328 n.). Rhetoric as a fine art consists in (mere) "eloquence and style," or, more expansively, a combination of "harmonious sound [*Wohllauts*] of speech and wealth [*Wohlständigkeit*] of expression for rational ideas" (*CJ* 5:327).

As for the *vir bonus dicendi peritus*, which Kant translates (nonliterally) as "the speaker without art but with full expression," such a speaker is apparently neither an orator nor a rhetorician. To put it more precisely, he employs "rhetoric" (*Rhetorik*) but in an "artless" way. And yet such artlessness can also be understood in two ways: either as "lack of guile" (or deliberate deceit) *or* as suggesting possession of an "insight" whose clarity and self-transparency transcends the semiconscious achievement of the poet.

In offering his own nonliteral translation, Kant avoids the error of which he is often accused (and of which Gottsched had indeed been guilty): namely, attributing the Latin phrase to Cicero.[77] Kant also manages to bring up Cicero's name in a broadly familiar context, given the widespread influence of Gottsched's writings. Kant thereby gives added emphasis to his concluding point: Cicero's failure, in his own "speeches to the people," to live up to his own professed oratorical ideal.

Kant alludes to that failure when he notes in the previous sentence that "both in Athens and in Rome [the art of the orator] reached its highest level at a time when the state was hastening toward its destruction and a truly patriotic way of thinking was extinguished" (*CJ* 5:328 n.) It is not *all* ancient speeches to the people,[78] then, but those in which the practice of rhetoric had reached its height and when the spirit of freedom had vanished, that arouse in Kant a private "feeling of disapproval." This detail will prove important to his later discussion (at *CJ* 5:355–56) of the political achievement of the ancients.[79]

The ambiguous identity of the "speaker without art" gains added significance from the general importance Kant attaches to the problem of philosophic popularization[80] – a problem of which Kant was no doubt acutely aware

---

[77] The Latin phrase actually appears in Seneca and Quintilian (who attributes it to Cato the Elder).

[78] Compare Kant's earlier praise of ancient authors (at *CJ* 5:282).

[79] Compare the late reflection (*Refl-A* 15:495, #991): "If *Beredsamkeit* in a people mounts, the people is in decline, because it is overcome by illusion. The mere word 'Bereden' already expresses deception, not conversion [*überführen*] or conviction .... *Beredsamkeit* seeks to overpower the understanding by means of sensibility and semblance. Poetry brings pleasure merely to sensibility and leaves understanding free." Kant elsewhere contrasts *Beredsamkeit* so understood with *Beredheit* – a kind of *Wohlredenheit* – that is praiseworthy even if not always strictly truthful (as with, e.g., the *Beredheit* by which women naturally control men). See also *Anth* 7:304, 306 and *Refl-A* 15:701, #1485; 840, #3444; but compare, for example, *Relf-A* 15:421, #952. On Kant's use of "*Beredsamkeit*" when speaking of rhetoric of a morally harmful kind, see Stroud (2014).

[80] See, for example, *P* 4:261; *G* 4:409; *MM* 6:206; *JL* 9:47.

given his confessed lack of "talent" for "lucid exhibition."[81] Indeed, Kant's long-standing dispute with Garve, well-known champion or proponent of the so-called Popularphilosophie and translator of Cicero's *On Duties*, turned, it might be argued, on the "true" meaning of "popularity."[82]

But the potential targets of Kant's argument concerning both rhetoric and the speaker without art do not end here. In *The Social Contract* and *On the Origin of Languages,*[83] Rousseau had distinguished between nonrational *persuasion* and rational *conviction*, arguing that the former rather than the latter was the key to successful legislation.[84] Rational conviction, as he saw it, necessarily rests on individual self-interest; as such, it can never sustain the bonds necessary for a just and healthy communal life. Kant's favoring of conviction over persuasion absorbs Rousseau's critique of reason, which in the latter's view is always instrumental, while also radically transforming it through a reassessment of the true ends of reason. Hence, "rational conviction" no longer means – as it did for Rousseau – adherence to the dictates of a reason that ultimately serves natural inclination. At the same time, Rousseau gave Kant a new appreciation of the creative possibilities of the imagination, an appreciation that (partly thanks to Herder's provocations)[85] had achieved new philosophic depth by the time Kant assumed the task of writing a systematic Critique of Taste. In addressing the issue of rhetoric, then, Kant is engaged in a complex dialogue not only with both the classical tradition and Rousseau, the thinker singularly responsible for his own earlier philosophic "revolution," but also with other German figures of significance, including Herder, who had similarly been influenced by Rousseau.

With these complications in play, this much is clear: Kant distinguishes *ars oratoria* understood as "dialectic" *both* from *"Wohlredenheit,"* or excellence in speech (understood as a species of "fine art"), *and* from that expression "without art" which is necessary and sufficient in the "courtroom and the pulpit" (*CJ* 5:327) or wherever "pronouncement of the law" wishes to be "effective."[86] Indeed, that speaker as here described, (i.e., as one who "has under his control"

---

[81] *CPR* (B xliii).

[82] See, for example, *JL* 9:47, in which Kant links true popularity with study of both ancient authors (including Cicero's philosophic writings) and moderns, including Hume and Shaftsbury, who Garve particularly favored. Garve, who translated Cicero's *On Duties* into German on Frederick the Great's request, was the author of many influential works and the translator of Burke's *Philosophic Inquiry into the Origins of Our Idea of the Sublime and Beautiful* and Adam Smith's *Wealth of Nations*. His reviews of the first edition of the *Critique of Pure Reason* are thought to have prompted Kant's writing of the *Prolegomena*. Part One of Kant's essay on *Theory and Practice* is an explicit response to Garve.

[83] *Social Contract*, Book Two, ch. 7 (Rousseau, 1959–1995:3:383); *Discourse on the Origin of Languages* (Rousseau, 1959–1995:5:383, 428). See also Kelly (1987).

[84] Rousseau (1959–1995:5:428).   [85] See Zammito (1992).

[86] See, for example, *G* 4:389: "[moral philosophy] gives ... laws a priori, which no doubt still require judgment sharpened by experience, partly ... to provide access to the will of the human

both "clear insight into things" and "language in all its purity and richness" and also, by virtue of a "fruitful imagination capable of presenting his ideas," a "lively, heart[felt] share in the true good") would seem to be the ideal speaker *as such*, at once *equaling* the poet in the fruitfulness of his imagination and *exceeding* him in control over language and clarity of insight (*CJ* 5:328 n.).

Nor does Rousseau's own favored art – namely, music – escape Kant's critical eye. To be sure, from the standpoint of charm and movement, music, according to Kant, occupies the highest place (after poetry) and, as the art of tone, exceeds poetry in universality (*CJ* 5:328). For whereas the communicability of poetry is dependent on knowledge of a particular language,[87] music expresses a tonal "language of affects" whose communicability does not rest on the semantic meaning of words but instead exercises (*ausübt*) in its "full emphasis" (*ganzen Nachdrucke*) a "language of sensations" that is "universally comprehensible" (*CJ* 5:328).

The downside is that in this flux of tone nothing remains for the mind to contemplate (*denken ... nach*) (*CJ* 5:329). Accordingly, Kant tells us, music is "more enjoyment than culture" (*CJ* 5:328). Proceeding through "mechanical association, as it were," music barely rises to the level of fine art, and even this it does only insofar as it arouses "aesthetic ideas" of the simplest sort: maximally communicable because the accompanying play of thoughts is merely "the effects of, as it were, mechanical association" (*CJ* 5:328). Of all the fine arts, music least allows the mind to "feel its freedom" from the "laws of association." Accordingly, music's contribution to mental culture "occupies the lowest place" among the fine arts (*CJ* 5:329) and has "least value" from the standpoint of reason (*CJ* 5:328). Kant is here a far cry from Rousseau, whose Great Legislator speaks a "melodious language of freedom"[88] that is essentially musical and tonal. Indeed, music, according to Kant, whatever its claims to aesthetic universality, brings about an "animation" that is "merely corporeal," beginning with ideas but ending with "sensations of the body" (*CJ* 5:332).

The Analytic thus ends with an arresting set of claims. On the one hand, fine art of the highest rank – poetry – schematizes the supersensible (*CJ* 5:326), that is, makes it somehow sensibly accessible. On the other hand, rhetoric (in its pernicious form) and, in a lesser way, music, threaten to undermine the ends of reason: rhetoric, through deliberate interference with the power of reflection, and music through interruption, however unintended, of the business of thought and the freedom of others (*CJ* 5:330, 330 n.).

---

being and expression [*Nachdruck*] for carrying them out." See also *CPR* A589=B617; *CPrR* 5:25; *Anth* 7:165.

[87] Compare *Refl-A* 15:401, #917 from the late 1770s (also quoted in Dyck [2004]).

[88] The phrase is John Scott's (Scott, 1997).

4.2 The "Antinomy of Taste"

Rhetoric (of a negative kind), however, is not the only significant obstacle to human progress that Kant considers. At a certain civilizational stage, as Kant here insists, "mutually conflicting [*widerstreitende*] concepts . . . naturally and unavoidably arise" that challenge the "possibility" of taste as such (*CJ* 5:337). Such a challenge, moreover, seems most likely to arise with respect to taste that must be "acquired" (sometimes through strenuous study) and at times (like Kant's own) of recently increased social mobility in which the more and less urbane mingle with a freedom to which they were formerly unaccustomed.[89] At such a moment of emergent "rationaliz[ation]" (*CJ* 5:337) the *principle* on which judgments of taste are based becomes a matter of open debate; the question is not "is this beautiful?" but instead "on what grounds, if any, do you claim a right to the assent of everyone?" At moments such as these, the "lawfulness" of such judgments, and hence of their "inner possibility," become subject to a doubt that Kant's earlier deduction, which limited itself to free beauties of nature, is insufficient to dispel. Thus if taste is to be "saved," as Kant puts it, from an impasse that is as much practical as theoretical, the resulting "antinomy" of taste must first be resolved.

The antinomy of taste is harbored in two ordinary "commonplaces" (*Gemeinort[e]*).[90] According to the first, by which someone "without taste thinks to protect himself against reproach [*Tadel*]," "*everyone has his own taste*"[91] and hence, it seems, "no right to the necessary consent of others" (*CJ* 5:338). "*Tadel*" for Kant generally connotes disapproval, whether of oneself or others, that occupies a normative space falling between blame and regret.[92] And it is the term that he has used when emphasizing that aspect of aesthetic expectation (*ansinnen*) to which the word "should" properly applies, and in which "reproach" accordingly becomes appropriate. On what justified basis, then, can one be reproached for withholding one's assent to a judgment of taste (or reproach oneself, as with the untutored poet who ultimately improves his art [*CJ* 5:282])?

The second commonplace, "*there is no disputing [disputiren] about taste*,"[93] meets that question halfway by granting that judgments of taste are not, as with matters of disputation, subject to "proof" (*CJ* 5:338). The hypothetical aesthete, against whose "reproof" the person without taste seeks to defend himself,

---

[89] The classic study of "taste" as a response to these conditions (as reflected in Addison's *Spectator*, a model for Kant's own early *Observations*) is Habermas (1991).

[90] According to Zammito (1992:112), both commonly appeared in contemporary treatises on taste.

[91] A translation, presumably, of the French expression *chacun à son gout* (everyone to his taste).

[92] See, for example, *Anth* 7:146, 313; *CF* 7:86; compare *Refl-A* 15:318–19, #721.

[93] A translation, presumably, of the Latin phrase *de gustibus non disputandum*.

presumably knows better than to try to bring the novice around through disputation based on determinate concepts. But will he attempt to win the latter over
by other means or will he instead snobbishly dismiss him (as "*virtuosi* of taste"
are wont to do [*CJ* 5:298]) as irremediably crude? Will he grant, in other words,
that it is possible and appropriate to *enter into conflict* (*streiten*) about taste and
thereby "try to bring about unanimity . . . through mutual opposition [*wechsel-
seitigen Widerstand*]"? For this, however, there must be "hope of coming to
mutual agreement" and hence a "ground" for judgments of taste that is not
merely subjective (*CJ* 5:338). In short: If judgments of taste are to be "saved"
that hope must somehow find rational support.[94] But how is this possible, given
the apparent absence of concepts that might serve as a basis for mutual
agreement?

In response, Kant turns to a "third principle" that is "contained," as he puts it,
"in everyone's sense/meaning" (*jedermanns Sinne*): namely, "*it is possible to
enter into conflict about taste*." By "conflict" (*Streit*), Kant means a kind of
opposition that is entered into not intransigently but with hope of an eventual
resolution.[95] And it is the possibility of conflict in that specific sense –
a possibility that is contained in "everyone's sense" and of which we all
therefore have some (limited) awareness – that Kant now attempts to establish
more firmly by teasing out, and overcoming, its seemingly contradictory implications. These implications are themselves imbedded in the twin "peculiarities"
of taste (subjectivity and universality) (*CJ* 5:281, 284)[96] that rule out disputation (in the first case), while also demanding the assent of others (in the second).

The *thesis* states:

> The judgment of taste does not ground itself on concepts, for otherwise one
> could dispute (*disputiren*) over it, which is to say, to decide by proofs.

The *antithesis* counters:

> The judgment of taste grounds itself on concepts, for otherwise one could not,
> despite its variety, enter even into conflict (*streiten*) over it, which is to say,
> make claim to the necessary assent of everyone.

---

[94] Interpreters often miss this crucial point, along with the necessary role of "hope" in making possible
the culturally productive "conflict" between the more and less urbane Kant means to promote. An
exception is Allison (2001:237), who goes on to ground Kant's resolution on the "rational idea" of
"beauty." It is difficult, however, to see how beauty could be a rational idea, given the latter's
definition as a "concept made up of notions" (i.e., of pure concepts of the understanding) (*CPR*
A320=B377). Unlike rational ideas, which are attributable, if only heuristically, to all rational beings
as such, "beauty" is valid, according to Kant, "only for human beings," that is, for beings who are
animal as well as rational (see *CJ* 5:210). Accordingly, Kant never speaks of an "idea" of beauty other
than in a "normal" or partially empirical sense (*CJ* 5:233).

[95] For similar uses of "*streiten*," see, for example, *CPR* A420=B448 and *CF*.

[96] For an extended treatment, see Makkai (2020).

The resolution hinges on the two senses in which "concept" can be taken –
that is, *either* as meaning a "determinate concept," which the subjectivity of
taste precludes, *or* as a "concept [of reason]" that is "indeterminate" and
"indeterminable [theoretically]" (*CJ* 5:339) but that supports the "hope" of
coming into eventual agreement by means other than objective proof (and that
is thus compatible with both sides of the argument).

What then is the indeterminate and (theoretically) indeterminable concept
that can ground such a hope? The short answer: a concept of that which "can be
regarded as" the "supersensible substrate of humanity [*Menschheit*]" (*CJ*
5:340). For, as Kant puts it, while appeal to a determinate concept would
contradict the thesis, and hence the necessary subjectivity of taste,

> All contradiction falls away if I say: the judgment of taste grounds itself in
> a concept (of a general ground of the subjective purposiveness of nature for
> the power of judgment), but through which with regard to the object nothing
> can be known or proven ... ; while through the same concept it acquires
> validity for everyone (to be sure as a singular judgment immediately derived
> from intuition), because its determining ground perhaps lies in a concept of
> that which can be regarded as the supersensible substrate of humanity
> [*Menschheit*]. (*CJ* 5:340)[97]

The larger issue here is how aesthetic judgments of exemplary artistic beauty,
a taste for which must be "acquired," can make a necessary claim to the assent of
others – a question that Kant's earlier "deduction" had conspicuously left
hanging.[98] The "ground" to which judgments of acquired taste can appeal
includes a presumption on which *all* judgments of taste rely: the subjective
purposiveness of nature for the general power of judgment. But judgments of
acquired taste must *also* appeal to (the indeterminate concept of) a "supersensible
substrate" of "humanity" that transcends mere nature.

Kant draws his peculiar understanding of "humanity" (i.e., *Menschheit*, as
distinguished from *Humanität* [*CJ* 5:355]) largely from Rousseau, who had
showed in his two *Discourses* "the unavoidable conflict of culture with the
nature of the human species qua *physical* species," as Kant puts it *Conjectural
Beginnings* (*CB* 8:116). But Rousseau, according to Kant, did not leave matters
there; he also sought in *Emile* and the *Social Contract* "to solve the harder
problem of how culture must proceed in order to develop the predispositions of

---

[97] Kant's doubly qualified repair here to the supersensible is thus not the "desperate flight" into
metaphysics for which it is sometimes taken but merely the minimum that is necessary to support
the "hope" required if "conflict" about taste (and with it, the ongoing "progress of culture" [*CJ*
5:283]) is to be possible at all. Compare Allison (2001:246) and Guyer (1997:240).

[98] Compare Guyer (2000:xxxv).

humanity [*Menschheit*] as a *moral* species to their determination [*Bestimmung*]," so that the two "no longer conflict" (*CB* 8:116).

Menschheit so conceived is a problematic whole whose actualization is the never-to-be-fully-completed task of human history. As such, it stands in direct contrast to the concept of the human species offered by Herder in his famous *Ideas for the Philosophy of the History of Humanity*, which had accused Kant of an "Averroistic" understanding of "humanity" that privileged a merely nominal universal over a reality residing solely in the individual. Kant had pointedly replied that by "the human species" he meant to signify not merely a shared "mark," but rather a "*whole* of a series of generations" stretching toward the infinite that ceaselessly approximates the "destiny" (*Bestimmung*)[99] that "runs along beside it" (*HR* 8:65). The *Critique of Judgment* offers the critically rigorous aesthetic response to Herder that Kant's earlier brief essay had anticipated in its playful (and largely Rousseauian) attribution of the historical origins of taste to women's sexual refusal (*CB* 8:113).

The "subjective freedom" of aesthetic judgment is reconcilable, then, with its pretension to a universal standard of correctness on the following terms: that the latter claim appeals, with all the modesty of a "perhaps," to the concept of an underlying source of harmony between nature and the power of judgment broadly construed.[100] That one can say as much without challenging the autonomy of taste resolves the crisis that threatened, both conceptually and socially, the very possibility of a regulative "idea" of common sense on which judgments of acquired taste might rely.

4.3 Semblance and Deception

The practical effect of Kant's earlier Analytic was mainly on the individual, whose powers of aesthetic discrimination (e.g., of beauty from mere charm) were thereby refined and reinforced. The practical effect of the Dialectic, in contrast, is also social. By lifting the "deception" to which the "semblance" of contradiction gives rise (*CJ* 5:340), resolution of the antinomy of taste removes the arrogance and/or defensiveness that otherwise threatened to impede culturally progressive class conflict (as it were) between the more and less refined.

At the same time, resolution of the antinomy also promotes Kant's larger, architectonic aims: namely, to "seek out the unifying point of all our faculties a priori in the supersensible" even "against our will," and thereby make "reason

---

[99] I translate "*Bestimmung*" here as "destiny" to capture the intended sense of an end or complete determination of the species toward which human development is (or should be) heading; compare *IUH* 8:18.

[100] See also Kant's elusive reference (at *CJ* 5:341) to the riddle (of the Sphinx), whose answer is, presumably, "the human being." Compare *JL* 9:25.

self-concordant [*mit sich selbst einstimmig zu machen*]" (*CJ* 5:341). At stake is thus not only the possibility of an a priori principle of taste suitable to moments of civilizational crisis (like the present), but also the unity of reason itself.

But if this is so, then the purposive unity of all our faculties, as expressed "without [intentional] purpose" through artistic genius, may bear a special relation to the "unriddling" of the concept of humanity – an unriddling for which the "subjective principle of taste," as Kant here insists, provides the only available key (*CJ* 5:341).[101] For that unity serves as a mediating link between the three ideas of the supersensible: first, the "supersensible in general without further determination as the substrate of nature"; second, the "very same as principle of the subjective purposiveness of nature for our faculty of know-ledge"; and, third, "the very same as principle of the ends of freedom and principle of the harmony of nature with these ends in the moral [realm]" (*CJ* 5:346). This unity is purposive, moreover, not only with respect to imagination and understanding (as with judgments of taste in their most elemental form) *but also* to reason, with whose "judgment" taste must finally harmonize if aesthetic pleasure in fine art is to endure (*CJ* 5:326).

Hence the peculiar significance of the art(s) of speech. Heretofore, we have been presented with three sorts of "semblance": one beautiful and necessarily deceptive, one beautiful and incapable of deceiving, and one neither beautiful nor necessarily deceptive. The first sort of semblance is associated with perni-cious rhetoric (*Beredsamkeit*), the second with fine art (especially poetry), and the third with a philosophic exercise of speech (*sagen*) and naming (*heissen*) (*CJ* 5:340) that transforms, through assumption of a critically "transcendental" standpoint, a counter-purposive antagonism into a "conflict" that is purposive both theoretically and historically. The appropriate antidote to rhetoric is not poetry (alone), as it might earlier have seemed, but a philosophical critique of the faculty that judges them both.

And yet a further critical task awaits, for the resolution of the antinomy does not yet provide what Kant had promised (at the end of #40): a justification or "deduction" of an a priori principle of taste that does not merely *posit* common sense (as with judgments of free beauties of nature) as a constitutive condition of objective experience as such, provided one is not a skeptic (*CJ* 5:239), but also *demands* it as a goal to be achieved "as if it were a duty." Indeed, Kant signals as much when he refers, in what follows, to a (second) "deduction" that is "on the right track" (*CJ* 5:346) and hence, by implication, both *different* from that offered in #38 and still unfinished. Such a principle would especially apply

---

[101] Compare Geiger (2021), according to whom *all* fine art is for Kant a presentation of the rational idea of humanity; but see Halper (2020).

to representations of artistic beauty – although at a high stage of culture, natural beauty too "can generally be regarded as the *expression* of aesthetic ideas" (*CJ* 5:319).[102] Whereas the "savage" notices mere shape and play, the civilized observer, to whom nature (like the poet) "speaks" (*CJ* 5:302), may well note and take pleasure in a "higher [expressive] meaning" (*CJ* 5:225).

The justification of an a priori principle of taste that must be *acquired*, and hence whose absence is properly an object of *reproach* (by oneself or others) is, then, still underway. Such a justification would help to explain "how it is that the feeling in the judgment of taste is expected of everyone as if it were a duty" (*CJ* 5:296). And, crucially, it would also provide taste's cultivation with the guidance necessary (*CJ* 5:240) to avoid the twin shoals of "re-barbar[ization]" (*CJ* 5:282–83) and a (false) "idealization" (*CJ* 5:433; cf. *CJ* 5:240).

5 The Politics of Beauty

We approach the final sections of Part One with completion still pending of a deduction applicable to judgments of acquired taste. We earlier learned that "if we could assume that the mere universal communicability of feeling must already involve an interest for us" we could explain taste's duty-like claim on the assent of others (*CJ* 5:296) and thereby better understand the universality and necessity that such judgments may properly assert.

The stipulation that this mere communicability must *already* involve an interest meant that it should arise from aesthetic judgment *as such* and without the mediation of either an empirical interest (which would depend upon our "natural inclination to society" [*CJ* 5:297–98]) or a moral interest (which would presuppose the very moral cultivation that the refinement of taste manifestly jeopardizes [*CJ* 5:298]).

What we are also still seeking, then, is an interest capable of supporting a transition *from* sensual pleasure *to* moral satisfaction. Such an interest must: (1) not challenge the disinterestedness of judgments of taste; (2) arise with respect to judgments of *artful* as well as natural beauty; and (3) link our natural inclination to society with a susceptibility to moral feeling while remaining distinct from each.

5.1 Beauty as Symbol

Section #58 ("On the idealism of purposiveness of both nature and art as the sole principle of aesthetic judgment") not only unites the two kinds of taste Kant has heretofore treated more or less separately; it also provides an important clue as

---

[102] See also Halper (2020). Such a reading (by emphasizing "can") resolves what would otherwise be a flagrant textual inconsistency.

to their underlying similarity. Judgments of taste (be it of natural or artful beauty) are "rational" rather than "empirical" and at the same time "ideal" rather than "real" (*CJ* 5:347). That is to say, they do not affirm the objective existence of a purpose to conform with the needs of our power of judgment but look upon this harmony as merely serendipitous, that is, as purposive without purpose (*CJ* 5:347). And this is true not only of the purposiveness of nature but also the purposiveness of art (for the artist of genius cannot articulate either to himself or others the rule on which he relies). Aesthetic judgment differs in this respect from the teleological judgment that Part Two will specifically address, in which the purposiveness in question (e.g., that of plants) is regarded as objective (*CJ* 5:347).

It is thus striking that Kant introduces his discussion of "Beauty as Symbol of Morality" in #59 with two cases in which the purposiveness in question is "objective": namely, a "bare machine" (e.g., a hand mill) as the symbol of a despot, and an ensouled body as the symbol of a monarch ruling "in accordance with inner popular laws" (*nach inneren Volksgesetzen*) (*CJ* 5:352). We will have reason to return to these examples shortly; for now, however, it is important to bring out the features of symbolization, as Kant here defines it, that these cases are intended to illustrate: namely, an analogical relation that turns on a common principle of causation and hence a common "rule of reflection" that obtains even when the items themselves are entirely dissimilar (*CJ* 5:352). How, then, might these examples help us better understand the symbolizing relation between beauty and the morally good, granted that the purposiveness in question is subjective rather than objective? The question is all the more pressing given Kant's declarative insistence on the importance of such symbolization in explaining how (or, rather, under what conditions) judgments of *both* natural and artful beauty can properly lay claim to the assent of others as if it were a duty:

> Now I say: the beautiful is the symbol of the morally good [*Sittlich=Guten*]; and also only insofar as one has this in view [*in dieser Rücksicht*] (that of a relation, that is natural to everyone, and that everyone also expects of others as a duty) does it please with a claim to the assent[103] of everyone, whereby the mind simultaneously is conscious of a certain ennobling and elevation [*Erhebung*] over the mere receptivity of pleasure through sensible impressions and also esteems [*schätzt*] the value of others following a similar maxim in their [power of] judgment. (*CJ* 5:353)

A central difficulty in interpreting this passage arises from its seeming inconsistency with the deduction at #38, which had *already* established that

---

[103] "Determination" (*Bestimmung*) in the first edition of the *Critique of Judgment*.

claim with respect to free beauties on the basis of a purposiveness for cognition generally. And yet, as we subsequently learned, the claim to universality of a taste that must be *acquired* can be "saved" from contradiction only by appealing to the indeterminate and (theoretically) indeterminable concept of that which "can be regarded as" the supersensible substrate of humanity. And it is the latter sort of taste, I would argue, that Kant has in mind in the above quoted passage – a taste whose claim to universal validity rests not only on the constitutive conditions of cognition insofar as it can be communicated, but also on taste's connection "whether near or distant" with ideas of reason.

In support of this reading I cite three pieces of textual evidence: first, limitation (whether explicitly or by implication) of Kant's earlier "epistemological" argument to pure judgments of free beauties of nature (see Section 1).

Second: Kant had earlier argued for the superiority, for purposes of presenting the moral aesthetically, of the sublime over the beautiful (in nature) on grounds that whereas beauty presents freedom as mere "play," the sublime presents it as "lawful business" (*CJ* 5:268). But we have subsequently learned that exemplary works must be "earnest" as well as playful (*CJ* 5:336). Might the beauty of such works – for example, in representing the sublime (*CJ* 5:325)[104] – symbolize morality more comprehensively than do free beauties of nature? But if this is so, then we have additional reason to conclude that beauty's symbolization of morality might especially apply to exemplary artistic beauty (and to natural beauties insofar as they arouse "aesthetic ideas"), whose claim to universality cannot be grounded in the basic conditions of cognition alone.

Third: the reading I propose would resolve the contradiction often claimed[105] between the literal meaning of the text (at *CJ* 5:353, which is sometimes taken to assimilate taste with morality[106]) and the deduction of taste at #38, which had grounded judgments of taste in the basic conditions of cognition of such. For any appearance of contradiction falls away once one attends to Kant's limitation of his earlier deduction to pure judgments of free beauties of nature. Here, however, he is referring to judgments of artful beauty (and other objects of acquired taste), whose pleasures cannot last, as he had earlier observed (*CJ* 5:326), unless they are combined, "whether closely or at a distance," with moral ideas. The "form" of artful beauty must be purposive, in other words, not only for cognition generally (as with free beauties of nature) but also for reason's

---

[104] Artworks cannot be judged sublime in their own right both because they cannot be judged to be both works of art and "formless" and because they provoke the empowerment of imagination, rather than its failure. See note 63 above and Abaci (2008).

[105] See, for example, Guyer (1979), neatly summarized by what Ameriks (1995) nicely calls the "Independence Claim."

[106] But compare Kant's earlier contrast between the (mere) "claims" of aesthetic judgment and the "commands" of moral judgment (*CJ* 5:267).

highest end (*CJ* 5:326). Nor need the passage (at *CJ* 3:23) be read as asserting the dependence of aesthetic judgment on morality. For the "*intelligible*" toward which "taste looks out," as Kant immediately clarifies, is that with which "our higher faculties of cognition [must] harmonize" lest "manifest contradictions" arise between the "nature"[107] of those faculties and "the claims of taste," and artful beauty soon cease to please (*CJ* 5:353, 326). In sum: our pleasure in fine art, if it is to be lasting, must "harmonize" with our "higher" ends, albeit without undermining the "autonomy" of taste by expressing a direct interest in achieving them.[108]

The "intelligible" toward which taste here "looks out" (*CJ* 5:353) resembles, in this respect, the indeterminate concept of the "substrate of humanity [*Menschheit*]"[109] on which Kant's resolution of the antinomy of taste had earlier turned. Humanity so conceived surely involves the "nature" of our "higher faculties of cognition"; but it also includes our "[natural] inclination to society" – albeit only insofar as our "sociability" is also "*suitable*" to our humanity [*Humanität*]" (*CJ* 5:355; cf. *CJ* 5:433). And that indeterminate concept thereby lifts – at least potentially – the interest to which our "sociability" gives rise beyond the merely empirical (cf. *CJ* 5:296–97). But in so doing it also open up the possibility of an *intellectual interest in the beautiful* that specifically applies to *objects of fine art (and natural beauty insofar as it gives rise to "aesthetic ideas")*.

As regards the latter: artistic works without spirit (i.e., that do not arouse aesthetic ideas that resonate with the ideas of reason) quickly become tiresome (*CJ* 5:326), not least – as we here learn – because the animation of the imagination is impeded rather than enhanced by its relation to the other higher cognitive faculties. Thus, while fine art should not consciously aim to be edifying (as with the "academic" verses, perhaps, of "a certain poet" [*CJ* 5:316]) it cannot fail, in cases of exemplary genius, to elicit in the well-trained judge a certain openness to moral possibility, rooted in the analogous autonomy of aesthetic judgment and the "judgment of reason" (*CJ* 5:326).

---

[107] On the extended meaning of nature here, see also *CJ* 5:314.

[108] See, for example, Guyer (1993:318) and Zuckert (2007:377–78).

[109] On the importance of the concept of humanity, see also Dobe (2018) and Stoner (2019). Neither dwells, however, on the tension *within* human "sociability" (i.e., between sociability as a merely animal inclination and sociability as a rational determination or destiny [*Bestimmung*]) that renders any concept of its substrate "indeterminate," putting pressure on *us* to do as much as each of us can to overcome that tension. Compare in this regard Kant's earlier references to "sociability" (*Geselligkeit*) insofar as "it rests on empirical rules" (*CJ* 5:213) and as the object of a "natural inclination" that is "empirical and psychological" (*CJ* 5:218) to his more elevated use of the term in #41: If one "grants" (as he there puts it) that human beings are not only "naturally" driven toward society, but also "creatures destined for society," then "*sociability*" is not *merely* natural (in a strictly empirical sense) but also "a property belonging to humanity [*Humanität*]" (*CJ* 5:296–97).

Kant's specific mention of esteem in relation to judgments of taste (at *CJ* 5:353) both recalls, and contrasts with, his earlier discussion of the "beautiful soul" who was also said to merit "esteem" (*CJ* 5:300). He had there apparently subsumed any interest that artful (as distinguished from natural) beauty might arouse under the heading of "empirical interest in the beautiful" (*CJ* 5:297).[110] Kant has subsequently provided, however, an analysis of exemplary works of art that surpass natural beauty not only in the perfection of their form (*CJ* 5:299) but also in their contribution to "the cultivation [*Cultur*] of [*all*] the forces of the mind for sociable communication" – a cultivation in accordance with our "higher ends," as he has now shown, even if it cannot aim at them directly without ceasing to be "purposive without purpose," that is, no longer merely aesthetic.[111]

5.2 The King's Speech Revisited

Kant's two examples – namely, a mechanism and a biological organism as respective "symbols" of a despotism and a monarchy with strong republican features – call to mind his earlier reference to Frederick the Great. Which sort of ruler – a despot or a monarch ruling in a "republican spirit" – might Frederick have represented in Kant's mind, and, as he might expect, that of the alert reader? To be sure, in *Perpetual Peace* Kant appears to allow that Frederick *might* have been the latter. As Kant there states, with respect to the distinction between a despotism and a monarchy, it is at least "possible" for the latter "to adopt a way of governing in conformity with the *spirit* of republicanism," as with Frederick II, for example, who at least *said* that "he was only the highest servant of the state" (*TPP* 8:352–53; emphasis in the original).

That Kant would later publicly question Frederick's sincerity on this score has already been noted. For as Kant writes in the *Anthropology*, while "*publicly* professing to be merely the highest servant of the state," the "great king's" inadvertent private "confession" could not "conceal" his true opinion (*Anth* 7:333 n.). As Kant also states, by way of explanation:

> For the moral predisposition of the human being is used politically by legislators, a tendency that belongs to the character of the species. However, if morals do not precede religion in this discipline of the people,

---

[110] But compare his qualification of that claim (at *CJ* 5:299–300): The beautiful soul prefers natural beauty to works of art "that sustain vanity and at best social joys" (*CJ* 5:300); Kant says nothing there about whether that preference would also hold for works of genius.

[111] Compare Allison (2001:265), who reads Kant's reference to duty (at *CJ* 5:253) as invoking our imperfect duty toward self-perfection, which, on Allison's argument, includes cultivation of a taste for natural beauty in order to make oneself more susceptible to moral feeling.

then religion makes itself master [*Meister*] over morals, and statutory religion
becomes an instrument of state authority [*Gewalt*] (politics) under *religious
despots*; an evil that inevitably puts out of tune [*verstimmt*] and misguides
character by governing it with *deception* [*Betrug*] (called statecraft
[S*taatsklugheit*]). (*Anth* 7:333 n.)

Although Frederick, in marked contrast with his successor, may have
publicly allowed freedom of religion, his deceptive self-representation as
the "first servant of the state" marks him as equally guilty of ruling
despotically, that is, "in a manner contrary to a republican constitution"
(*Anth* 7:333 n.).

Frederick's dishonesty may also help account for why Kant, in calling
Frederick "the great king," avoided the other sobriquet he commonly bore:
namely, the "philosopher king." For as Kant also notes in *Perpetual Peace*: that
"kings should philosophize or philosophers become kings is not to be expected,
but it is also not to be wished for," since, pace Plato's *Republic*, "the possession
of authority [*Gewalt*] inevitably corrupts [*verdirbt*] the free judgment of reason"
(*TPP* 8:369).

If further confirmation were needed that the "state as mechanism" analogy
was more applicable in Kant's mind than the "state as organism" to Frederick
II's reign, one might consider Frederick's own widely read eulogy for La
Mettrie, the infamous author of *L'homme machine*, to whom Frederick had
offered political refuge and whose unqualified "materialism" the king had
thereby implicitly endorsed. In thus appearing as a full-bored defender of
a mechanistic account of human life (and hence the view that human beings
are nothing more than complicated machines), Frederick posthumously champions a philosophic position that Kant will decisively reject in Part Two of the
Critique of Judgment, in his own critical justification of the use of teleological
principles in the investigation of biological organisms. In the course of that
Critique Kant will favorably compare such organisms to the recent "transformation of a great people" (in implicit comparison with the "great king"). After
stating that an organized being "is not ... a mere machine: for that has only
a *motive* [*bewegende*] force, while an organized being has *formative* [*bildende*]
force, and indeed one that it communicates [*mitthelli*] to matter [*Materlen*]" (*CJ*
5:374) – an "inscrutable" property that is perhaps best described as an "*analog
of life*" (*CJ* 5:375) – Kant then notes:

One can conversely illuminate a certain association [*Verbindung*], albeit one
that is encountered more in the idea than in reality [*Wirklichkeit*], through an
analogy with the immediate ends of nature mentioned above. Thus with
a recently undertaken total [*gänzlichen*] transformation [*Umbildung*] of
a great people [*grossen Volks*] into a state the word *organization* often very

56 *The Philosophy of Immanuel Kant*

aptly served for the setting up of the magistracies, etc., and even the total state body [*Staatskörper*]. For every member [*Glied*] should freely be determined in such a whole [*Ganz*] not only as a means but at the same time also as an end, and, insofar as it cooperates in the possibility of the whole, its position and function should also be determined by the idea of the whole. (*CJ* 5:375 n.)

Writing at a time when the French monarchy had not yet fallen and the National Assembly had indeed recently voted to continue to grant Louis XVI a veto, Kant might easily have regarded France as a constitutional monarchy in which the king ruled in accordance with the "inner laws of the people." His adoption here of "organic" terms lifted almost verbatim from Sieyès' influential *What Is the Third Estate?*,[112] which appeared near the beginning of 1789, gives added weight to the supposition that the "great people" that Kant has in mind here is French rather than American,[113] whose status as a single nation (rather than a federation of states) was arguably still unclear.

What retrospective light might these examples shed on the proper use of "hypotyposis," and hence on rhetoric,[114] which should never be used, according to Kant – even in its more innocuous form (i.e., as "the art of eloquence" rather than "persuasion") – either "for the courtroom," before "parliament," or "from the pulpit" (*CJ* 5:327, 328 n.), that is, wherever "it is a matter of civil laws concerning the rights of individual persons, or of the lasting determination and instruction of minds to correct knowledge and conscientious observation of their duty" (*CJ* 5:327)? Here, the "artless" speaker – who has in his control "clear insight in matters of language in all its purity and richness," along with "full expression," and an "imagination" apt for the "fruitful presentation of his ideas, " as well as a "lively participation of the heart" for the true good (*CJ* 5:328 n.) – has a decisive advantage not only over the rhetorician but also over the poet. Kant thereby suggests one way in which the cultivation of taste along critical lines, and concomitant reduction of the seductive power of rhetoric, might indeed serve reason's higher ends.

At the same time, in making his own critically "scientific" (*CJ* 5:355) (and hence artless) use of "hypotyposis" (cf. *CJ* 5:352) Kant assumes the role of – or at least clears the ground for – a "vir bonus dicendi peritus," who can address the people "without art" and as an undeceiving alternative to the king who claimed to be their servant. In so doing, Kant also critically revisits his earlier treatment, circa 1784, of cultural and civil progress as sufficiently assured by Frederick's

---

[112] Compare Sieyès (2002:52). The first addition was published in January 1789, followed by two more in the same year.
[113] Compare Pluhar (1987:54 n.).
[114] "Hypotyposis" was a standard rhetorical term, dating back at least as far as Cicero, and meaning "to make the absent vivid." See Vasaly (1993:90); compare Kant (*Refl-L* 16:131 [#1830]).

"mechanical" way of governing (*WIE* 8:37) under the slogan: "argue [*räsonniren*] as much as you will ... ; only obey!" (*WIE* 8:41). Instead, Kant offers an alternative mode of aesthetic "conflict" [*Streit/streiten*] partly modeled on the exemplary speech of the ancient Greeks and Romans (*CJ* 5:282–83).

5.3 The "Modus" of Taste

The Appendix to Part One that follows ("On the Methodology of Taste") omits the doctrine of method (*Methodenlehre*) that would normally accompany the critique of a faculty; for where "beautiful art" is concerned (*CJ* 5:355) there can be no "method" of teaching (*Lehrart*) (which would require explicit rules)[115] but only a "manner" [*Mannier, modus*].[116] Instead, the teacher must bring principles of taste to mind without prescribing them, and seek to awaken the student's own efforts toward expressing the "idea"; he must then subject those efforts to the "sharpest criticism" without inhibiting the student's freedom of imagination or otherwise stifling his genius (*CJ* 5:355).

In an earlier reference to the "*modus aestheticus*," Kant had addressed two opposing errors on the part of young or otherwise untrained artists: "copying" (*Nachschäffung*) on the one hand and "mannerism" (*Manieren*) on the other. The first consists, as he there put it, in an attempt to imitate those bold departures from taste that are "of merit" (*Verdienst*) solely in the genius (*CJ* 5:318); the second consists in privileging one's own idiosyncrasies solely to distinguish oneself from the "common" [people] [*dem Gemeinen*] (but without spirit – i.e., "conform[ity] to the idea") (*CJ* 5:319).The behavior of the mannered artist who aims at "mere ... originality" (*CJ* 5:318) confuses "spirit" with abhorrence of "the common ranks" (another meaning of *der Gemeine*).[117] And he clings to *his* idea (as in Frederick's verse) rather than seeking to express the universal.

That the Methodology of Taste is specifically concerned with the cultivation of taste for "fine art" gives added emphasis to the distinction – one that I have

---

[115] Compare Matherne (2019:10–16).

[116] On the distinction between manner and method, see also *JL* (9:139): "All cognitions, along with a whole of cognitions, must be commensurate with a rule (that without a rule is without reason [*Regellosigkeit ist zugleich Unvernunft*]). But this rule is either one of manner (free) or one of method (compulsion)." In the *Critique of Pure Reason* Kant had described the "manner" of the good as "beautiful semblance" by which human beings are already partly moralized under the "coercion" of "discipline" (*CPR* A748=B 776). Kant's presentation in the third *Critique* of the "discipline" of taste as "mannered" rather than "methodical" (and hence free rather than coercive) allows, as we shall see, for a more nuanced account of the relation of civilization to moralization than he was earlier able to provide.

[117] In his earlier treatment of "common sense," Kant had stressed the distinction between "common" (*gemein*) and "vulgar" (*vulgare*) or "encountered everywhere," the latter possessing neither "merit" nor "advantage."

been stressing throughout – between the elementary taste in which even "savages" share and the taste for fine art that accompanies, for better or for worse, the rise of civilization. It is the latter sort of taste that gives rise, for reasons both theoretical and historical, to an "antinomy" along with the accompanying need for a new "deduction." And it is the latter taste that can and must be "acquired," as distinguished from a taste for free beauties of nature, which only requires that one be introduced to them when one is young (and, presumably, before one's natural taste has had a chance to be corrupted) (*CJ* 5:326). To acquire a correct taste for fine art, on the other hand:

> One must have regard for a certain ideal, which art must always have before its eyes, although in execution it is never fully achieved. Only through the arousal of the student's imagination to becoming commensurate with a certain concept by the aforementioned inadequacy of the expression of the idea, which the concept itself does not achieve because the idea is aesthetic, and through sharp criticism, can the student be prevented from taking . . . examples . . . as . . . archetypes [*Urbilder*] for imitation rather than models . . . that are subjected to a higher norm and his own judging, [thereby] smothering the genius together with the freedom of his own imagination even in its lawfulness, absent which no fine art, or even a correct taste . . . for judging it is possible. (*CJ* 5:355)

One is here reminded of Kant's earlier discussion of the "ideal of beauty," possessed by the judge no less than the artist, and whose higher norm is the "idea of the highest [moral] purposiveness" (*CJ* 5:236). That thought returns in Kant's discussion, in the paragraph that now follows, of the "propaedeutic to all fine art" in which "the forces of the mind" are purposively united in accordance with "the sociability appropriate to our humanity":

> The propaedeutic to all fine art, insofar as it makes its concern the highest grade of its perfection, seems to lie not in precepts but instead in cultivation [*Cultur*] of the forces of the mind through that foreknowledge [*Vorkenntisse*] that is called the *humaniora*; presumably because *humanity* [*Humanität*] signifies, on the one hand, the universal *feeling of participation* [*Theilnehmungsgefühl*], and on the other, the capacity [*Vormögen*] to be able universally *to communicate* [*mittheilen*] most inwardly, which properties, bound together, constitute the sociability appropriate to our humanity [*Menschheit*], by which it is distinguished from animal limitedness [*Eingeschränkheit*]. (*CJ* 5:355)

Three things here bear noting: First, the foreknowledge in question is especially associated with study of the "humanities"– that is, the literature of ancient Greece and Rome. Second, it is presumably so called because it involves both "participation/sympathy" and the "capacity to communicate most inwardly." Third, these two qualities in combination facilitate a sociability appropriate to our *Menschheit*, as distinguished from the "natural inclination toward society" (earlier treated under the heading of "empirical interest in the beautiful" [*CJ* 5:297]), that is, directed *solely* by an interest in sensual pleasure.

Beginning with the second point: Kant's inclusion within his definition of *"Humanität"* of both *"Theilnehmung"* and *"Mittheilung"* incorporates sublimity (cf. *CJ* 5:292) and beauty (cf. *CJ* 5:272) within a single aesthetic faculty (as befits a fine art capable of representing the sublime beautifully [*CJ* 5:325]). Kant's earlier treatment of ancient models (*CJ* 5:282–83) had not entirely ruled out the possibility of progress beyond that earlier standard. As he there put it: just as an "example of virtue or holiness," established in "history," does not make "dispensable" (*entbehrlich*) the "autonomy of virtue out of one's own and original idea of morality [*Sittlichkeit*], or transform [*verwandelt*] it into a mechanism of imitation," so *"succession,"* rather than "imitation," is "the correct expression for all influence that an exemplary author can have on another" (*CJ* 5:283). The classics are to be admired, on Hume's account, because they exemplify empirical rules that summarize "what has been universally found to please in all countries and in all ages," as witnessed by the enduring reputation of these works down through the centuries (Hume, 1985). The classics are exemplary, for Kant, in a different way: namely, as sites of a law-giving to the people (*CJ* 5:282) that is consistent with the aesthetic autonomy of the subject.

Moreover, in describing those ancient authors as a kind of "noble class among writers," Kant implicitly allowed that later writers of genius might proceed more "popularly" – less as lawgivers *to* the people than as lawgivers *through* the latter's own living language. That not all works of exemplary genius, but only those deemed "classics," must be written in "dead" languages (*CJ* 5:310) suggests that modern examples might in this respect have a certain advantage, if not in their endurance over time, then in their immediate capacity to spiritually enliven the widest possible audience.

To be sure, the language of learned Roman authors was not "dead" to their own immediate audience (although the weight in this case of Greek, for them a learned tongue, may have especially suited their works for classic status in their own time). Indeed, the aesthetic superiority of the ancient authors, at this point in the argument, would seem to lie less in their intrinsic merit than in the fact that their languages happen to have been preserved as learned, thereby fixing meanings otherwise subject to the flux of changing verbal fashion (*CJ* 5:283).

That there is more to their exemplarity becomes clear, however, in the following section (#60), which links the peculiar aesthetic status of the classic *humaniora* to certain distinctive *political* characteristics of both their peoples and the age in which they lived:

> The age as well as the peoples [*Völker*] in which the keen drive toward *lawful* sociability, through which a people constitutes an enduring commonwealth [*gemeines Wesen*] struggled with the great difficulties that surround the *difficult problem [Aufgabe] of uniting freedom (and hence also equality) with a compulsion [Zwang]* (more out of respect and subjection to duty than fear); such an age and such a people must have first discovered the art of reciprocal communication of the ideas of the most educated [*ausgebilde-testen*] part with the cruder [*roheren*] part, the attunement [*Abstimmung*] of the breadth and refinement of the former with the natural simplicity and originality of the latter, and in this way [Art], that mean between the highest culture and a sufficient nature, which also constitutes the correct standard, for which no universal rule can be given, for taste as universal human sense [*allgemeinen Menschensinn*]. (*CJ* 5:355–56; emphasis added)

Before the ancient Greeks and Romans could constitute themselves as an enduring commonwealth and thus proceed toward solving the "difficult task" of uniting freedom with compulsion (more out of respect than fear), they had first to discover an "art" that both resembles and differs from the art of rhetoric as earlier described. Unlike modern speeches before the court and from the pulpit – and unlike those of Cicero himself during Rome's time of political corruption (*CJ* 5:327–28 n.) – artful expression there consisted in "reciprocal communication" between the more educated and the cruder, thereby combining the former's "breadth," "refinement," and "highest culture" with the latter's "simplicity," "originality," and natural "sufficien[cy]."

Before the problem of combining freedom with compulsion could be productively addressed, in other words, a communicative art had first to be found that avoided the defects of deceitful manipulation to which even Cicero proved prone and that marks the limits of Rome's own political achievement. Art needed to proceed politics, and what in the former case was a "discovery" was merely a lucky guess or happy accident in the latter, without the rational guidance of either a morally purified Christianity[118] or a critically chastened philosophy.

As to the future propaedeutic role of those ancient writings, Kant leaves the matter open:

> A later age will make such models dispensable with difficulty: because it will always be further from nature and, ultimately, without having enduring examples of it, will hardly [*kaum*] be in a position to form [*machen*]

---

[118] Compare *CPrR* (5:127 n.).

> a concept of the fortunate uniting in one and the same people of the lawful
> compulsion of the highest culture with the force and rightfulness [*Richtigkeit*]
> of a free people that feels its own value. (*CJ* 5:356)

That this politically crucial concept was still available, even without recourse to
the ancients, would become thematic in later writings concerning, for example,
both the "spirit-rich" French (*CJ* 7:85) and the honest Lithuanians, a people
Kant also describes as both "original" and as capable of "feeling their own
value" (*PF* 8:441).[119] What is most remarkable for current purposes is Kant's
reiterated pairing of (on the one hand) lawful compulsion with "the highest
culture" and (on the other) "force" and "rightfulness" with a "freedom" and
"originality" that refinement without critical insight is all too prone, as we have
seen, to stifle.

    Kant may be responding here to an influential passage from Rousseau's *Emile*
warning that commerce and enlightenment might soon destroy whatever remains
of "peoples" in their "original genius" and "simplicity" (Rousseau [1955–95,
4:853–54]). That the opposition between enlightened reason and a patriotic way
of thinking may be less dire, given the proper aesthetic education, than Rousseau
implies – an implicit theme, as I have claimed, of Kant's Critique of Taste
throughout – now emerges into the open, as well as posing a still unanswered
question: Can the classics be surpassed?

    That question is given sharper focus by the formal resemblance between the
ancient "art of reciprocal communication," on the one hand, and exemplary
works of artful beauty, on the other, each of which combines (albeit in its own
way) freedom and originality with the discipline necessary for "the highest
culture." As genius is to taste, so were the ancient popular classes to the more
educated – exemplary products of genius recapitulating, in this respect, the
serendipitous discovery that made the ancient republics possible.

    One aspect of an answer is, however, already clear: The "true propaedeutic
for the grounding of taste" is not a study of the *humaniora*, however indispensable it may seem, but "the development of moral ideas" and the "cultivation of
moral feeling," activities in which the moderns have, it would appear, a decisive
advantage (*CPrR* 5:127 n.).

> But since taste is in its foundation [*im Grunde*] the faculty for judging the
> sensualization of moral ideas (by means of a certain analogy of reflection over
> both) ... from which, along with increased receptivity to moral feeling, ...
> [aesthetic] pleasure derives ..., and declares itself valid for humanity as
> such ... ; so ... the true propaedeutic for the grounding of taste is the

---

[119] See also Kant's observation that, among the fine arts, poetry owes most to genius and is least in
need of "precept or example" (*CJ* 5:326).

> development of moral ideas and the cultivation of moral feeling; for only when sensibility is brought into accord with this can genuine taste assume a determinate, unalterable form. (*CJ* 5:356)

In this puzzling final passage, Kant seems to assert *both* the dependence of moral cultivation upon taste (insofar as taste makes us more receptive to moral feeling) *and* the dependence of taste upon moral cultivation (in definitively securing taste's claim along with a stability of form that is inalterable).[120] In what might be called a virtuous historical circle, taste opens us to moral ideas and in so doing validates and stabilizes itself retroactively, enabling us to learn from what proceeds us without unduly limiting, and thereby stifling, our own originality.

Taste as here understood is no longer the fledgling capacity, grounded in a "constitutive" norm of aesthetic common sense (*Gemeinsinn*), to which the deduction at #38 applied, but is a developed faculty (*Vermögen*), critically enlightened about its own a priori principle, and actualized by way of a "universal human sense" (*algemeinen Menschensinn*) that must be brought about by us (cf. *CJ* 5:240).

It is instructive to compare this concluding paragraph with an early forerunner, whose general theme – namely, the relation of aesthetics and morality by way of politics and history – the present conclusion partly echoes:

> If finally we cast a few glances at history, we see the taste of human beings like a Proteus. . . . The ancient . . . Greeks and Romans showed clear marks of a genuine feeling for the beautiful as well as the sublime, in poetry, painting, architecture, lawgiving, and even morals. The rule of the Roman emperors changed [that] noble . . . and beautiful simplicity into the magnificent and then false shimmer [*Schimmer*] of what still survived. (*OFBS* 2:255)

With the "complete destruction of the state," even this false shimmer (along with its "rhetoric" and "poetry") vanished, leaving it to the barbarians, with the aid of "warlike adventurers and monks," to perpetuate the Gothic taste that replaced the "ancient simplicity of nature" with unnatural and fantastic forms (*OFBS* 2:255). Fortunately:

> the human genius lifted itself out of an almost complete destruction by a kind of palingenesis, so that we see in our times correct taste blossom in the arts and sciences as well as with regard to the moral, and there is nothing more to be wished for than that the false shimmer [*Schimmer*] that so easily deceives not distance us unremarked from the noble simplicity,[121] but especially, that

---

[120] Kant had anticipated this claim (at *CJ* 5:326).

[121] A term especially associated with Johann Winkelmann, whose *Thoughts on the Imitation of Greek Works in Painting and Sculpture* appeared in 1755.

the undiscovered secret of education should be torn away from the ancient delusion, in order to early raise the moral feeling in the breast of every young world citizen to an active susceptibility, lest all refinement merely amount to the fleeting and idle enjoyments of judging with more or less taste what goes on around us. (*OFBS* 2:256)

In both the pathos and the expectation of this early passage, published when Kant was only forty, and with his major academic career still ahead of him, one hears not only the echo of Rousseau (and Winkelmann) but also an anticipation of Kant's later claim, in *Idea for a Universal History*, that civilization, insofar as it "is not grafted onto a moral disposition" is nothing more than "shimmering [*schimmerendes*] misery" (*IUH* 8:26). By 1790, when he completed the final version of the *Critique of Judgment*, Kant had reasons to be both more hopeful and more apprehensive.

5.4 Beyond the Politics of Taste

Where, then, does #60 finally leave us with respect to "the idea" of a common sense "yet to be acquired," as Kant had earlier put it, "so that one's expectation of universal assent" is itself merely a "demand of reason to produce it" (*CJ* 5:240)? He had there asked whether the "should" of taste might not "signify only the possibility of coming into agreement about this." The resolution of the antinomy regarding the principle of taste had shown that such an expectation is not self-contradictory on its face. But this resolution had also rested, as we have seen, upon a "hope" of coming into agreement about taste – a hope that could be secured only by appealing to an indeterminate concept of the supersensible substrate of "humanity."[122] As to the *reality* of such a substrate (and with it the ultimate solubility of the problem of uniting freedom and coercion), nothing has yet been shown.

The "methodology" of Part Two (Critique of Teleological Judgment) takes up both taste and art anew, as part of a more general consideration of the ultimate end of nature – including human nature – as a teleological system (cf. *CJ* 5:433, 474). And it includes an extended treatment of another theme that is relevant both politically and aesthetically: namely, the distinction, in matters theological–political, between rhetorical "persuasion" (*CJ* 5:462) and rational conviction (*CJ* 5:463, 477).

Kant's repeated comparison, in the latter's favor, of persuasion to conviction is, as I have argued, an implicit criticism of Rousseau, for whom civil freedom and the full development of reason are incompatible (inasmuch as reason ultimately dictates self-interest rather than virtuous identification with the

---

[122] See also Düsing (1990:90).

general will). For Kant, on the other hand, the individual socialized through the persuasive rhetoric of a "Great Legislator" is not genuinely free, not least where persuasion takes a religious form. Hence the peculiar importance of distinguishing, as a matter of philosophic "duty" (*CJ* 5:462), between physico-teleology, which issues only in persuasion (*CJ* 5:482 n.), and rational theology proper (*CJ* 5:472). For the mere "semblance" of conviction to which the former gives rise can lead, if not carefully guided, to an abhorrence of investigation (*Prüfung*) itself (*CJ* 5:462). Indeed, Kant will devote the final pages of the *Critique of Judgment* to consideration of the delicate relation between physico-theology (whose popularity is indisputable) and an ethico-theology that prompts rationally groundable "conviction" (*CJ* 5:463). At its best, physico-theology makes "capable of being felt" (*CJ* 5:484) the need for a theology that can "adequately determine the concept of God for reason's practical use"; at worst, however (and without the clarifying aid of critical philosophy) it presents itself under the false guise of rational proof, encouraging mental passivity (and the inclination toward reason's mechanical use rather than its spontaneity under laws).

Earlier in Part Two Kant had provided a critical answer to both a "Spinozistic" materialism (that would reduce life to matter) and a Herderian hylozoism (that would make matter live) (*CJ* 5:392–93). He thereby offered a viable alternative to materialistic "fatalism" that did not, in the Herderian manner, breach the boundaries of reason itself and thereby mistakenly confound philosophy and poetry (cf. *HR* 8:60). In so doing, Kant also provided a reflective principle allowing one to regard "culture" as both an "ultimate end of nature" (*CJ* 5:431) *and* a product of free human beings. In his new appreciation for the teleological duality of human "sociability" (as a "natural inclination" and/or as "appropriate to our humanity") Kant both enriches and goes beyond the mechanical analogies on which he had rested his progressive hopes in *Idea for a Universal History* and *What Is Enlightenment?*[123]

Culture, as Kant now conceives it, both internalizes and transforms the principle of dynamic opposition that had characterized his earlier account of history, which had modeled itself more on a mechanical cosmogony than on organic processes, for which he still lacked the necessary a priori principle. Culture in a "positive" sense (as Kant now puts it) – that is to say, as the "subjective formal condition" of the bringing forth of the aptitude of a rational being "for any ends at all" including those of freedom – permits one to regard nature as an organized whole, albeit one that also requires a final (moral) end that it is up to human beings to realize (*CJ* 5:436). This *positive* culture (or culture of "skill") gives rise to the "necessary elements" of culture – namely,

---

[123] See, for example, *IUH* (8:27).

science and art; but it also presupposes a social inequality that relegates "the greatest number" to "lives of oppression, bitter toil and little enjoyment," though with "much [higher] culture gradually spreading" to them (*CJ* 5:432). At this stage, "the tendency to the dispensable destroys the indispensable," and progress gives way to "luxury" or to desires that are both unstable and potentially insatiable. At such a moment, "the plague on both sides becomes equally mighty – on the one hand through outer violence, on the other through inner insufficiency"; and yet this "glittering misery" is "bound up with the natural predispositions of the human species" and thus promotes nature's end, if not our own: namely, the establishment of that "civil society" in which "reciprocally conflicting freedom is opposed by lawful power [*Gewalt*]" (*CJ* 5:432; cf. *IUH* 8:26).

Thus far Kant has hardly gone beyond the account of "a-social sociability" in *Idea for a Universal History*. But he now supplements the "positive" culture of "skill" with a "*negative*"[124] culture (*CJ* 5:432) of "discipline" (newly understood),[125] and hence a *second* pathway to moral ends not featured in that earlier essay:

> As concerns the discipline of inclinations, for which the natural predispos-
> ition aiming at our determination as an animal species is entirely purposive
> but that makes the development of humanity [*Menschheit*] very difficult;
> nature displays even in regard to this second requisite of culture a purposive
> striving toward a formation [*Ausbildung*], which makes us receptive to higher
> ends than nature itself can deliver. [To be sure] the preponderance of ills with
> which we are shaken by the refinement of taste to the point of its idealization
> [*Idealisirung*] ..., because of the insatiable host of inclinations that are
> thereby aroused, cannot be contested [*bestreitet*]. (*CJ* 5:433)

The transition from animality to rationality – both for the individual and for the species as a whole – is problematic, as Kant allows both here and elsewhere.[126] And yet even with respect to this fraught moment, nature, as he now adds, proves purposive by "winning out ever more," thanks to science and *fine* art, against the "crudity and impulsivity" of the inclinations of "enjoyment," thus "prepar[ing] human beings for a mastery in which reason has full authority [*Gewalt*]" (*CJ* 5:433).

---

124 Emphasis added.

125 Compare *CPR* (A709–10=B 737–38), where "discipline" was identified with compulsion (*Zwang*) rather than training (*Zucht*), and *opposed* to culture (*Cultur*) rather than constituting its second, and equally important, branch. Imagination no longer needs only a coercive discip-line (as in the *Critique of Pure Reason*), but is instead susceptible to the "free" discipline of a higher "training" that merely clips its feathers (*CJ* 5:319).

126 See *CB* (8:113, 116–17, 117 n.); on the Rousseauian provenance of Kant's formulation of the problem, see also *Anth* (7:326).

By "idealization" Kant here has in mind, I would suggest, the privileging of the communicability of a feeling over the feeling itself – at first with a view to the approval of others and eventually in the name of an "idea" of universal communicability that has lost nearly all relation to the pleasure actually felt (cf. *CJ* 5:297). This reading is supported by Kant's sole other critical use of "idealization" – namely, in the *Critique of Pure Reason*, where it signifies a transcendent use of reason in which "ideas" break free of their proper, regulative role and assume an illusory "constitutive" reality of their own (*CPR* A469=B497; A474=B502). The idealization of taste involves a similar error (*CJ* 5:297; and pp. 23–24 above). Our discontent with pleasures unless we can enjoy them "in community with others" is initially innocuous enough – that is, a purposive expression of our natural inclination toward society. Eventually however, civilization makes "beautiful forms," along with the "empirical interest" they arouse, almost the chief work of "refined inclination"; so that finally the value that is attributed to the pleasure is almost entirely eclipsed by the "almost infinitely" greater value that is attributed to the idea of its "universal communicability" (*CJ* 5:297; cf. *CJ* 5:326). Civilization, as we saw earlier, here stands at a crossroads: between the blending (*zusammenschmelzen*) of aesthetic pleasure with mere enjoyment (*CJ* 5:298) or the "flowing together" (*zusammen-fleissen*) of "the sense of each with all" in pure aesthetic satisfaction (*CJ* 5:240). The Critique of Taste aims to nudge civilization back onto its proper track – not least, by restoring subjective feeling to its rightful place as the first "moment" of beauty. An "idea of ... universal communicability" that has been emptied of almost all pure aesthetic content must be replaced by a regulative "idea of [a] common *sense*" to be "brought about" in accordance with the demands of reason.

We have at last arrived at an "interest" arising from aesthetic judgment a priori (cf. *CJ* 5:298) that is capable of spanning the divide between sensible pleasure and moral satisfaction, and hence at a regulative principle in accordance with our "higher ends" that is consistent with (but not exhausted by) the constitutive criteria of aesthetic judgment generally. Our satisfaction in the prospective "existence" of a "common sense" congruent with a "general human sense" is compatible with both the disinterestedness of aesthetic judgment and the latter's rationally approvable result.

In bringing that interest explicitly to light, moreover, Kant raises the "art of reciprocal communication" between the more and less refined to a higher level of inner transparency than was possible in ancient Greece and Rome.[127] The "glittering misery" to which class inequality has heretofore given rise can now

---

[127] See also Düsing (1990:85–86).

be offset, and perhaps one day canceled entirely, through a mutual *Humanität*, that is, the "universal feeling of participation" and "the capacity to communicate one's inmost self" that constitute the sociability that is not only "natural" to us as an empirical species (*CJ* 5:297) but also "appropriate to our *Menschheit*" (*CJ* 5:355).

At the same time, a completed deduction (or one completable by us) of the *regulative* principle of taste proves to be inseparable from the *teleologicus rationalis* and accompanying attention to "the essential ends" of reason that is included in Part Two under the heading of the "ultimate end of nature." It is these essential – but not yet moral – ends to which, I venture, Kant had earlier alluded in speaking of a regulative principle of taste guided by our "higher ends" (*CJ* 5:240) Those ends, which he describes elsewhere as consisting in the "culture of reason,"[128] are the point of intersection (as distinguished from merger) between nature's ultimate end, which consists in "culture,"[129] and the "final end" of reason, which is moral. Those ends give rise, in turn, to an "interest" in the cultivation of forces of the mind that, too, is neither strictly *moral* nor merely *sensual* and thus capable of furnishing, both theoretically and practically, the sought for transition between the agreeable and the good without breaching the crucial critical distinction between ethics and aesthetics.

The Critique of Taste not only furnishes the "employment of taste" with the rationally grounded "guidance" for which Kant had earlier called (*CJ* 5:297); it also allows for a gentler leap between sensible enjoyment and moral feeling than proved possible on the basis of empirical interest alone (*CJ* 5:298). Although a critically chastened taste for objects of artistic beauty cannot, as such, depend on any interest, either empirical or intellectual, it gives rise to one, thereby reconciling, however precariously, the conflictual features of human "sociability" – one rooted in our "natural inclination to society," the other adequate to the demands of our "humanity." In so doing, the faculty of teleological judgment bears reflective witness to the supersensible substrate of "humanity" to whose related "principles" (of nature, taste, and morals respectively) Kant had earlier alluded (*CJ* 5:346).

In short: thanks to the critical incorporation of a republican model of aesthetic communication, and the peculiar "interest" that accompanies or flows from it, the refinement of taste can promote, rather than obstruct, the ongoing progress of culture. Kant's critique thereby fulfills, both theoretically and practically, the second aim mentioned in #41: namely, "exhibit[ion] of a mediating link in the chain of faculties a priori, on which all lawgiving must depend," in service to the *Critique of Judgment*'s larger, systematic goals.

---

[128] *G*:396; *CPR*:B-xxx, A817=B845.   [129] Düsing (1990:90).

6 Summary and Conclusion

The *Critique of Judgment* not only brings Kant's critical project formally to a close; it also, as I have argued, aims to intervene politically (and morally) at a time when the immediate republican promise of the French Revolution was seemingly at its height. That moment would soon pass, giving way to terror abroad and political and religious repression at home. Still, the a priori principle of judgment presented and defended in the Critique of Taste enabled Kant to integrate his "*Lieblingsidee*" of human history within a systematic critical framework for the first time.

That this a priori principle found its justification in a deduction of pure judgments of taste indicates the importance of judgment of free beauties of nature, in particular, to that larger systematic goal. But Kant does not end his treatment of taste with the deduction of that constitutive principle but also seeks to establish a regulative principle of taste suitable to the judgment of artistic beauty. Such a principle would not only guide the acquisition and refinement of taste in a manner consistent with the higher ends of reason; it would also give rise to, without depending on, an intellectual interest in the beautiful: namely, the bringing about of a universal common sense applicable to artful beauty; and it would thereby provide the transition from agreeable pleasure to moral satisfaction for which our empirical interest in the beautiful proves inadequate.

Kant's ensuing discussion of fine art aims to reconcile his earlier analysis of beauty as "purposive without purpose" with the intentional character of art as such. Although judgment of a work of genius necessarily involves a concept of what something is to be, it does not depend upon that concept in the manner characteristic of adherent beauty, which is conditional on the satisfaction of an end other than aesthetic pleasure. Instead, imagination creates another nature that extends beyond the limits of the understanding through the production and communication of "aesthetic ideas" that elicit the motion of reason itself.

At the same time, the contestability of a taste that is not "original and natural" but must be "acquired" inevitably gives rise to an "antinomy" over principle, pitting the necessary subjectivity of taste against its claim to universality. Kant's critical resolution rests, in turn, upon a "hope of coming into eventual agreement" based on the "indeterminate concept" of the "supersensible substrate of humanity." Such a subjective concept provides a common point of reference that does not call upon, or otherwise involve, objective proof. But it also falls short of securing the objective possibility of a common sense to be brought about by us (as called for in Kant's earlier description of a regulative principle of taste in accordance with the higher ends of reason).

Kant takes up the latter task when he returns to the themes of history and culture in the concluding sections of the Critique of Teleological Judgment. For, as he there argues, we are indeed permitted to assume, albeit only for purposes of reflection, the existence of such a supersensible substrate of humanity and hence of the ultimate unifiability of our animal and rational natures, thanks in part to the "discipline of imagination" consistent with the latter's freedom that the Critique of Taste makes possible. Kant had good reason to believe, as he completed the final pages of the third *Critique*, that "reciprocal communication" between the more and less refined on a new, critically enlightened basis might well be imminent. If so, the critical tension between "civilization" and "moral-ization" (as Kant had put it in *Idea for a Universal History*) – though not altogether resolved – would at least be eased, perhaps decisively.

Kant's own confidence in the even partial adequacy of an "aesthetic" solution to central difficulties of political life would soon wane in the face of heightened theological–political challenges, beginning with the new Religious Edict issued shortly before the appearance of the *Critique of Judgment* in April 1791. Kant's *Religion within the Boundaries of Bare Reason* (1793) supplemented the "ethico-theology" of the third *Critique* with a more pessimistic appraisal of the root of human evil.[130] Whereas in that earlier work Kant had assumed the role of *viri bonus dicendi peritus* by replacing physico-theology with ethico-theology (i.e., mere "persuasion" in religious matters with rationally grounded "conviction" or its ever nearer approach), any such attempt, as he now saw it, would require prior confrontation with popular passivity and lassitude along with a deeper investigation (under the title of "radical evil") of its ground in the human propensity to *self*-deception.

Others, however, including above all Schiller, would take up Kant's hint in #83 as to the possibilities of an "aesthetic education of humanity."[131] Thus inspired, they would go on to call for and create new, nationally based literary and artistic works drawing on the "spirit" of the "people" as mediated by their enlightened interpreters and champions. Even Kant, toward the end of his public life and with the challenges of both religious suppression and revolutionary terror receding, could present history as turning on an instance of universal participation and inmost sympathy.[132] In that expressive recollection of the Revolution in its more innocent early days one senses a chastened republican spirit reviving once again.

---

[130] For a detailed discussion, see Shell (2009).

[131] Schiller (1954). (The *Letters* [*Briefe*] appeared in 1795).

[132] See *CF* (7:85–86) and Shell (2021).

References

A Note on Translation and Citations of the Works of Kant

References to Kant's work, with the exception of the *Critique of Pure Reason*, follow volume and page of the German Academy edition: Kant's Gesammelte Schriften, Königlich Preußischen Akademie der Wissenschaften, later the Deutschen Akademie der Wissenschaften zu Berlin (Walter de Gruyter [and predecessors], 1902–). Translations are generally my own; I also occasionally draw on the Cambridge edition of the *Critique of the Power of Judgment* (2002), edited and translated by Paul Guyer (with Eric Matthews).

I have used the following abbreviations for Kant's works:

Anth	Anthropology from a Pragmatic Point of View
CB	Conjectural Beginnings of Human History
CF	Conflict of the Faculties
CJ	Critique of Judgment
Corr	Correspondence
CPR	Critique of Pure Reason
CPrR	Critique of Practical Reason
G	Groundlaying of the Metaphysics of Morals
HR	Review of Herder's "Ideas for a Philosophy of the History of Humanity"
IUH	Idea for a Universal History with a Cosmopolitan Intent
JL	Jaesche Lectures on Logic
MFNS	Metaphysical Foundations of Natural Science
MM	Metaphysics of Morals
OFBS	Observations on the Feeling of the Beautiful and the Sublime
On a Discovery	On a Discovery in Which Any New Critique of Pure Reason Is to Be Made Superfluous by an Old One
P	Prolegomena to Any Future Metaphysics
PF	Postscript of a Friend
Refl-A	Reflections on Anthropology
Refl-E	Reflections on Ethics
Refl-L	Reflections on Logic
Rem	Remarks in "Observations on the Feeling of the Beautiful and the Sublime"

| *TPP* | Toward Perpetual Peace |
| *WIE* | What Is Enlightenment? |

Secondary Sources

Abaci, U. (2008). "Kant's Justified Dismissal of Artistic Sublimity," *Journal of Aesthetics and Art Criticism* 66 (3), 237–51.

Abbott, D. P. (2007). "Kant, Theremin, and the Morality of Rhetoric," *Philosophy & Rhetoric* 40 (3), 274–92.

Allison, H. (2001). *Kant's Theory of Taste*. Cambridge: Cambridge University Press.

Ameriks, K. (1995). "On Paul Guyer's Kant and the Experience of Freedom," *Philosophy and Phenomenological Research* 55 (2), 361–67.

Arendt, H. (1992). *Lectures on Kant's Political Philosophy*, ed. R. Beiner. Chicago, IL: University of Chicago Press.

Benjamin, W. (1968). "The Work of Art in the Age of Mechanical Reproduction," in *Illuminations*, ed. H. Arendt. London: Fontana, 217–52.

Burdick, S. (2010). *Kant and Milton*. Cambridge, MA: Harvard University Press.

Cazeaux, C. (2021). "Judging Contemporary Art with Kant," *Kantian Review* 26 (4), 635–52.

Chignell, A. (2007). "Kant and the Normativity of Taste: The Role of Aesthetic Ideas," *Australasian Journal of Philosophy* 85 (3), 415–33.

Clewis, R. (2009). *The Kantian Sublime and the Revelation of Freedom*. Cambridge: Cambridge University Press.

Clewis, R. (2018). "Beauty and Utility in Kant's Aesthetics: The Origins of Adherent Beauty," *Journal of the History of Philosophy* 56 (2), 305–35.

Costello, D. (2007). "Greenberg's Kant and the Fate of Aesthetics in Contemporary Art Theory," *Journal of Aesthetics and Art Criticism* 65 (1), 217–28.

Crawford, D. W. (1974). *Kant's Aesthetic Theory*. Madison, WI: University of Wisconsin Press.

Crowther, P. (2010). *The Kantian Aesthetic*. Oxford: Oxford University Press.

Dobe, J. K. (2010). "Kant's Common Sense and the Strategy of a Deduction," *Journal of Aesthetics and Art Criticism* 68 (1), 47–60.

Dobe, J. K. (2018). "Kant's a priori Principle of Judgments of Taste," in *Freedom and Spontaneity*, ed. K. Moran. Cambridge: Cambridge University Press, 66–86.

Dostal, R. J. (1980). "Kant and Rhetoric," *Philosophy and Rhetoric* 13 (4), 223–44.

Düsing, K. (1990). "Beauty as the Transition between Nature and Freedom in Kant's Critique of Judgment," *Nous* 24 (1), 77–92.

Dyck, C. (2004). "Spirit Without Lines: Kant's Attempt to Reconcile the Genius and Society," *Idealistic Studies* 7 (1), 151–62.

Ercolini, G. L. (2016). *Kant's Philosophy of Communication*. Pittsburgh, PA: Duquesne University Press.

Fugate, C. (2009). "Life and Kant's 'Critique of Aesthetic Judgment'," in *Akten des X Internationalen Kant-Kongressen*, eds. V. Rohden, R. R. Terra, and G. A. de Almeida. Berlin: De Gruyter, IV, 609–21.

Garsten, B. (2006). *Saving Persuasion: A Defense of Rhetoric and Judgment*. Cambridge, MA: Harvard University Press.

Geiger, I. (2021). "Kant on Aesthetic Ideas, Rational Ideas, and the Subject Matter of Art," *Journal of Aesthetics and Art Criticism* 79 (2), 186–99.

Ginsborg, H. (1991). "On the Key to Kant's Critique of Taste," *Pacific Philosophic Quarterly* 72 (4), 290–313.

Grimm, J. and Grimm, W. (1854 [1961]). *Deutsches Wörterbuch*. Leipzig: S. Hirzel Verlag.

Guyer, P. (1979). *Kant and the Claims of Taste*. Cambridge, MA: Harvard University Press.

Guyer, P. (1993). *Kant and the Experience of Freedom: Essays on Aesthetics and Morality*. Cambridge: Cambridge University Press.

Guyer, P. (1997). *Kant and the Claims of Taste* (revised edition). Cambridge: Cambridge University Press.

Guyer, P. ed. and trans. (with Eric Matthews). (2000). *Immanuel Kant: Critique of the Power of Judgment*. Cambridge: Cambridge University Press.

Guyer, P. (2005). *Values of Beauty: Historical Essays in Aesthetics*. Cambridge: Cambridge University Press.

Guyer, P. (2021). "Kant's Theory of Modern Art?," *Kantian Review* 26 (4), 619–634.

Habermas, J. (1991). *The Structural Transformation of the Public Sphere: An Inquiry into a Category of Bourgeois Society*, trans. T. Berger. Cambridge, MA: Massachusetts Institute of Technology Press.

Halper, A. (2020). "Rethinking Kant's Distinction between the Beauty of Art and the Beauty of Nature," *European Journal of Philosophy* 28 (4), 857–75.

Hume, D. (1985). *Essays Moral, Political, and Literary*, ed. Eugene F Miller. Indianapolis, IN: Liberty Classics.

Kalar, B. (2017). "The Ethical Significance of Kant's Sensus Communis," *Idealistic Studies* 47 (1/2), 43–58.

Kelly, C. (1987). "'To Persuade without Convincing': The Language of Rousseau's Legislator," *American Journal of Political Science* 31 (2), 321–35.

Kemal, S. (1992). *Kant's Aesthetic Theory: An Introduction*. New York: St. Martin's Press.

Kuehn, M. (2001). *Kant: A Biography*. Cambridge: Cambridge University Press.

Labio, C. (2004). *Origins and Enlightenment: Aesthetic Epistemology from Descartes to Kant*. Ithaca, NY: Cornell University Press.

Leeten, L. (2019). "Kant and the Problem of 'True Eloquence'," *Rhetorica* 27 (1), 60–82.

Lehman, R. (2018). "Lingering: Pleasure, Desire and Life in Kant's Critique of Judgment," *Journal of Speculative Philosophy* 32 (2), 217–42.

Longuenesse, B. (2006). "Kant's leading thread in the analytic of the beautiful," in *Aesthetics and Cognition in Kant's Critical Philosophy*, ed. R. Kukla. Cambridge: Cambridge University Press, 194–220.

Makkai, K. (2020). *Kant's Critique of Taste: The Feeling of Life*. Cambridge: Cambridge University Press.

Matherne, S. (2013). "The Inclusive Interpretation of Kant's Aesthetic Ideas," *British Journal of Aesthetics* 53 (1), 321–39.

Matherne, S. (2019). "Kant on Aesthetic Autonomy and Common Sense," *Philosopher's Imprint* 19 (24), 1–22.

McMahon, D. M. (2013). *Divine Fury: A History of Genius*. New York: Basic Books.

Murray, B. (2015). *The Possibility of Culture. Pleasure and Moral Development in Kant's Aesthetics* Malden, MA: Wiley-Blackwell.

Ostaric, L. (2017). "The Free Harmony of the Faculties and the Primacy of the Imagination in Kant's Aesthetic Judgment," *European Journal of Philosophy* 25 (4), 1376–1410.

Otabe, T. (2018). "*An Iroquois in Paris* and a *Crusoe on a Desert Island*: Kant's Aesthetics and the Process of Civilization," *Culture and Dialogue* 6, 35–50.

Pasquiere, R. (2020). "Toward a Reassessment of Kant's Notion of Rhetoric," *Studia Kantiana* 18 (2), 109–19.

Pluhar, W. S. ed. and trans. (1987). *Kant's Critique of Judgment*. Indianapolis, IN: Hackett Publishing.

Rogerson, K. F. (2008). *The Problem of Free Harmony in Kant's Aesthetics*. Albany: State University of New York Press.

Rousseau, J.- J. (1959–1995). *Oeuvres complètes* (5 vols.), eds. J. Starobinski et al. Paris: Galimard.

Rueger, A. (2008). "Beautiful Surfaces: Kant on Free and Adherent Beauty in Nature and Art," *British Journal for the History of Philosophy* 16 (3), 535–57.

Saville, A. (1987). *Aesthetic Reconstructions: The Seminal Writings of Lessing, Kant and Schiller.* Oxford, Blackwell.

Schiller, F. (1954). *On the Aesthetic Education of Man in a Series of Letters,* trans. R. Snell. New Haven, CT: Yale University Press.

Scott, J. (1997). "Rousseau and the Melodious Language of Freedom," *Journal of Politics* 59 (3), 803–29.

Shell, S. M. (2009). *Kant and the Limits of Autonomy.* Cambridge, MA: Harvard University Press.

Shell, S. M. (2010). "'Nachschrift eines Freundes': Kant on Language, Friendship, and the Concept of a People," *Kantian Review* 15 (1), 88–117.

Shell, S. M. (2021). "Kant as Soothsayer: The Problem of Progress and the 'Sign' of History," in *Kant and the Possibility of Progress*, eds. S. A. Stoner and P. T. Wilford. Philadelphia, PA: University of Pennsylvania Press, 115–34.

Shell, S. M. and Velkley, R. (2012) (eds.). *Kant's Observations and Remarks: a Critical Guide.* Cambridge, Cambridge University Press.

Sieyès, E. J. (2002). *Qu'est-ce que le Tiers état?* Paris: Éditions du Boucher.

Stoner, S. A. (2019). "Kant on Common-sense and the Unity of Judgments of Taste," *Kant Yearbook* 11, 81–99.

Stroud, S. R. (2014). *Kant and the Promise of Rhetoric.* University Park, PA: State University of Pennsylvania Press.

Stroud, S. R. (2015), "Kant, Rhetoric, and the Challenges of Freedom," *Advances in the History of Rhetoric* 18, 181–94.

Sweet, K. E. (2013). *Kant on Practical Life: From Duty to History.* Cambridge: Cambridge University Press.

Tonelli, G. (1966). "Kant's Early Theory of Genius (1770–1779)," *Journal of the History of Philosophy* 4 (2), 109–32; 4 (3) 209–24.

Trullinger, J. (2015). "Kant's Neglected Account of the Virtuous Solitary," *International Philosophical Quarterly* 55 (1), 67–83.

Tuna, E. (2018). "Kant on Informed Pure Judgements of Taste," *Journal of Aesthetics and Art Criticism* 76 (2), 163–74.

Vasaly, A. (1993). *Representations: Images of the World in Ciceronian Oratory.* Berkeley, CA: University of California Press.

Watkins, B (2011). "The Subjective Basis of Kant's Judgment of Taste," *Inquiry* 54 (4), 315–36.

Watkins, B. (2014) "Why Should We Cultivate Taste? Answers from Kant's Early and Late Aesthetic Theory," in *The Palgrave Handbook of German Idealism*, ed. M. C. Altman. London: Palgrave Macmillan, 126–43.

Wenzel, C. H. (2005). *An Introduction to Kant's Aesthetics.* Oxford: Blackwell.

Zammito, J. (1992). *The Genesis of Kant's Critique of Judgment.* Chicago, IL: University of Chicago Press.

Zinkin, M. (2006). "Intensive Magnitudes and the Normativity of Taste," in *Aesthetics and Cognition in Kant's Critical Philosophy*, ed. R. Kukla. Cambridge: Cambridge University Press, 138–61.

Zuckert, R. (2007). *Kant on Beauty and Biology*. Cambridge: Cambridge University Press.

Zuckert, R. (2008). "Kant's Double Justification of Taste," in *Akten des X Internationalen Kant-Kongressen*, eds. V. Rohden, R. R. Terra, and G. A. de Almeida. Berlin: De Gruyter, III, 775–86.

Acknowledgments

I should like to thank Robert Clewis, Michael Resler, Samuel Stoner, Jens Timmermann, and two anonymous readers for their generous assistance at various stages of this project.

Cambridge Elements ≡

The Philosophy of Immanuel Kant

Desmond Hogan

Princeton University

Desmond Hogan joined the philosophy department at Princeton in 2004. His interests include Kant, Leibniz and German rationalism, early modern philosophy, and questions about causation and freedom. Recent work includes 'Kant on the Foreknowledge of Contingent Truths', *Res Philosophica* 91 (1) (2014); 'Kant's Theory of Divine and Secondary Causation', in Brandon Look (ed.) *Leibniz and Kant*, Oxford University Press (2021); 'Kant and the Character of Mathematical Inference', in Carl Posy and Ofra Rechter (eds.) *Kant's Philosophy of Mathematics Vol. I*, Cambridge University Press (2020).

Howard Williams

University of Cardiff

Howard Williams was appointed Honorary Distinguished Professor at the Department of Politics and International Relations, University of Cardiff in 2014. He is also Emeritus Professor in Political Theory at the Department of International Politics, Aberystwyth University, a member of the Coleg Cymraeg Cenedlaethol (Welsh-language national college) and a Fellow of the Learned Society of Wales. He is the author of *Marx* (1980); *Kant's Political Philosophy* (1983); *Concepts of Ideology* (1988); *Hegel, Heraclitus and Marx's Dialectic* (1989); *International Relations in Political Theory* (1992); *International Relations and the Limits of Political Theory* (1996); *Kant's Critique of Hobbes: Sovereignty and Cosmopolitanism* (2003); *Kant and the End of War* (2012) and is currently editor of the journal *Kantian Review*. He is writing a book on the Kantian legacy in political philosophy for a new series edited by Paul Guyer.

Allen Wood

Indiana University

Allen Wood is Ward W. and Priscilla B. Woods Professor Emeritus at Stanford University. He was a John S. Guggenheim Fellow at the Free University in Berlin, a National Endowment for the Humanities Fellow at the University of Bonn and Isaiah Berlin Visiting Professor at the University of Oxford. He is on the editorial board of eight philosophy journals, five book series and *The Stanford Encyclopedia of Philosophy*. Along with Paul Guyer, Professor Wood is co-editor of The Cambridge Edition of the Works of Immanuel Kant and translator of the *Critique of Pure Reason*. He is the author or editor of a number of other works, mainly on Kant, Hegel and Karl Marx. His most recently published books are *Fichte's Ethical Thought*, Oxford University Press (2016) and *Kant and Religion*, Cambridge University Press (2020). Wood is a member of the American Academy of Arts and Sciences.

About the Series

This Cambridge Elements series provides an extensive overview of Kant's philosophy and its impact upon philosophy and philosophers. Distinguished Kant specialists provide an up-to-date summary of the results of current research in their fields and give their own take on what they believe are the most significant debates influencing research, drawing original conclusions.

Cambridge Elements ≡

The Philosophy of Immanuel Kant

Elements in the Series

A full series listing is available at: www.cambridge.org/EPIK